CROMWELL'S REVENGE
A TRUE STORY

PETER MCLOUGHLIN

MERCIER PRESS

First published in 2004 by
MERCIER PRESS
Douglas Village, Cork
Email: books@mercierpress.ie
Website: www.mercierpress.ie

Trade enquiries to CMD Distribution
55A Spruce Avenue, Stillorgan Industrial Park
Blackrock, County Dublin
Tel: (01) 294 2560; Fax: (01) 294 2564
E-mail: cmd@columba.ie

© Peter McLoughlin, 2004

ISBN 1 85635 436 9
10 9 8 7 6 5 4 3 2 1

A CIP record for this title is available
from the British Library

Mercier Press receives financial assistance from
the Arts Council/An Chomhairle Ealaíon

Printed in Ireland by ColourBooks Ltd

Contents

DEDICATED
TO MARY AND ROBERT

Introduction

In 1646, the Englishman Sir John Temple published his book *History of the Horrid Rebellion in Ireland*, an apparently factual account of the Irish uprising five years earlier. The publication contained gruesome and lurid accounts of how settler Protestants in Ireland were murdered, tortured and driven from their homes by the Irish.

> ... *The course they took was to seize upon all their goods and cattle, to strip them, their wives and children naked; and in that miserable plight, the weather being most bitter cold and frosty, to turn them out of their houses, to drive them to the mountains, to wander through the woods and bogs, and if they by any means procured any clothes, or but even ordinary rags to cover their nakedness, they were taken from them ...*
>
> *... Multitudes were presently killed in cold blood. Alas! Who can comprehend the fears, terrors, anguish, bitterness and perplexity of their souls, the despairing passion and consternation of their minds! What screeches, cries and bitter lamentations of wives and children, friends and servants, howling and weeping about them, all finding themselves without any manner of hope or deliverance.*

There was a certain element of truth to the allegations, though nothing on the scale suggested by Temple. But it inflamed English passions, and whipped up anti-Catholic and anti-Irish feeling. The Irish were seen as papist barbarians. The poet John Milton called them 'a mixed rabble, part papists and part savages, guilty in the highest degree of all these crimes ...' Avenging this genocide was a major motivating force for Oliver Cromwell when he brought his puritan army over to Ireland in 1649, believing the Irish to be 'barbarous and bloodthirsty'. The rebellion was seen as an act of popish treachery against Protestantism and civilsation. The Roman Catholic Church was blamed. In the words of the newsletter *Mercurius Hibernicus* the common people were 'stirred up by those seducing vipers, and firebrands of Hell, the bloody Jesuits and priests of the Antichrist Church of Rome'.

Cromwell's Revenge: A True Story tells how one 'Old English' settler family called Uniacke survived through this dark period of Irish history. The term Old English refers to those Anglo-Irish who retained their Catholic faith after the Reformation, while at the same time remaining staunch supporters of English rule in Ireland. They became increasingly marginalised as the Reformation progressed.* The authorities mistrusted them for being Catholic, and were quite happy to condemn and vilify them along with their Gaelic co-religionists. This group found itself in an even more unenviable position after the English Civil War. The fanatically anti-Catholic puritan forces of parliament had defeated and executed King Charles I, who, among other things, they despised for his sympathies towards Roman Catholicism. Those Old English who could not show 'constant good affection' towards the English state – meaning not having sided with the monarchy or Catholicism – forfeited their lands.

The Uniackes had been wealthy landowners in Co. Cork since the beginning of the fourteenth century, when the name first appears in public records. But it is quite possible the family came to Ireland in the twelfth century with Strongbow, as part of the Anglo-Norman invasion. Their estates were in the hinterland of Youghal, an important medieval walled town on the south coast, and a major port for the region.** After the Reformation, the English authorities in Youghal were generally tolerant of Catholics, who were allowed to hold public office and carry on trade. In the early seventeenth century, the Uniackes were listed as one of the 'Seven Denominations' in the town, making them among the wealthiest families in the area.

* *For a general account of the period see Appendix I: Turbulence and Change 1536–1708.*
** *For more details see Appendix II: A Historic Sketch of Youghal.*

After Cromwell had stamped out all effective opposition, the English parliament began its programme of land forfeiture, an ambitious scheme to remove Catholics from their estates and replace them with Protestant settlers. The Uniackes struggled to keep their properties, but to no avail. Yet, they did not suffer the bleak punishment of transplantation to Connaught in the west of Ireland, where many of those dispossessed of their lands were forced to move. Whether out of mercy or pragmatism the new Protestant landlords allowed the family to remain on the land, to manage the estate for the new master. Documents of their appeal to the Court of Claims, kept in the Armagh Public Library, show how this family had been reduced to tenants where they had been lords. After the restoration of the English monarchy, the Uniackes got their lands back.

The Uniacke story contains two of the great sources of conflict in Irish history: religion and land. Thomas Uniacke, heir to the estate, was a devout Catholic, and an unflinching supporter of the Stuarts, the family which had ruled England since the beginning of the seventeenth century. His younger brother, James Uniacke, converted to Protestantism since renouncing popery opened the way to Trinity College for him. James went on to become a wealthy lawyer in Dublin. The family division was deep and bitter. Yet, the two branches of the family remained on cordial terms, even when the country was once again shattered by war between the Catholic James II and his Protestant son-in-law William of Orange. But this was the time of the Penal Laws, a draconian system aimed at disenfranchising Catholic landowners, which always showed a bias towards heirs willing to renounce popery.

Cromwell's Revenge: A True Story is the result of three years of research. I am considerably indebted to one nineteenth-century genealogist, Richard Gordon Fitzgerald Uniacke, who was commissioned by the Uniackes to compile a family history. He transcribed many documents that were destroyed less than 30 years later in the Irish Civil War. His account goes back 600 years, with the genealogical record becoming quite substantial from the seventeenth century.

Fitzgerald Uniacke was a copious note-taker; some of his notebooks have survived and are in the possession of Jeremy Uniacke, who lives in Chichester, England. The manuscripts were rescued from an antique sale some years ago and given to the present owner. They are revealing, in that they sometimes tell more than the author wanted to publish – material the family would have been happier to censor. With the published and un-published writings of Fitzgerald Uniacke, existing genealogical evidence and other secondary sources and my own new primary research, I have been able to re-create this family's world, in one of the bleakest, most divisive chapters in Ireland's history.

BOOK ONE

1

'Troublesome Times'

The quill scraped across the vellum parchment, the obsidian-coloured ink forming a crisp if somewhat unsteady calligraphy, as Maurice Uniacke of Ballyvergin, set out his final instructions.

Present on that winter morning, 9 February 1648, were four close friends and confidantes: Fr Jasper Gallwan, Charles Oge McCarthy, Nicholas Miagh and Patrick Forrest. They were witness to an old man's frail efforts to save his family from destitution and oblivion.

Maurice Uniacke needed to retrieve or secure a trunk that had been deposited with his cousin, Robert Bluett, the suzerain of Killmallock in Co. Limerick, for safe-keeping two years previously. The trunk contained vital land documents and his last will and testament. If these items were destroyed so too would be the proof of a family pedigree dating back 400 years, and the entitlements of future generations of the Uniacke line. It was clear what had to be done:

> I do by these present nominate, constitute and appoint my well beloved cousin Richard Fitzgerald, Esquire, my brother (in law) Nicholas Meagh, and my brother Edmund Uniacke, to be overseers of my wife and children and this my last will and testament, and also to convert and dispose of all things herein expressed and declared to the best use and benefit of my said wife and children. Also I do appoint my said overseers to have a special care of my Writings and Evidences that concern my estate, which remain in one trunk by me left in the custody of my cousin Robert Bluett, Esqr, now suzerain of Killmallock, who left the same ... with his [illegible] Nicholas Kearny to be kept during these troublesome times, and my will is that my said cousin and my overseers – Richard Fitzgerald, Nicholas Miagh and Edmund Uniacke – shall procure or cause to lock with two keys apiece with

them, until such time as they may remove the said trunk from thence unto my wife's custody when the times are settled and if there be occasion to open the said trunk for to avail of my said children, and when my said son and heir before mentioned shall come to the age of twenty and one years, to deliver the said trunk and Evidences into his own hands and possession.

Maurice Uniacke also made a number of additions to his will, leaving 'one messuage or stone house' and 'several enclosures' of land to his newborn son, John. To his daughter, Joane, Maurice added an extra £130 to her dowry, bringing it to £230. Nor did he forget his sister, Christen Uniacke, leaving the 'sum of £5 sterling, to be paid to her in corn in the next year's crop as the market goes'. The same was bequeathed to his servant, Nell Bluett.

Maurice's son and heir, Thomas, was the main beneficiary of the original will, inheriting the bulk of the 600-acre estate and numerous houses, as well as some personal items, including a signet ring and a damask cloth.[*] The other sons – James, Edmond, Richard and John – all received comparatively modest amounts of property and land. Daughters Austace and Joane were assured their dowries of £200 and £230 respectively. Margaret Uniacke, who would outlive her husband by more than 20 years, had right to the estates during the minority of her children. If she were to remarry, a third of all 'estates and means' would pass to her. Nor did Maurice neglect his Christian duty: 20 shillings to the alms house, to be paid on each Easter Sunday for ten years; 40 shillings was to be distributed to the poor widows of Youghal; to Fr Jasper Gallwan, the secular parish priest, 30 shillings to pray for his soul. He requested that his mortal remains be wrapped in the habit of the Seraphical Order of St Francis, and buried in the ancestral tomb in South Abbey, outside the walls of Youghal.

Finally, Maurice Uniacke read the contents, so everyone knew what was involved. He rolled the parchment up tightly and fas-

* *For more details about the will see Appendix III*

tened it with the red wax seal. The witnesses signed the outside, and assured him that the document would be kept safely and its instructions carried out to the letter. They then left the old man alone in his study and left the Uniacke home. The task was daunting: to save the entitlement of this distinguished line of landed gentry – English, royalist and Catholic.

The oldest surviving reference to the family is in 1305, when a Bernard Unak appeared in the Plea Roll for Youghal. The surname appeared frequently throughout the centuries. Very little is known about its origin, but one story said it derived from the word *Unicus*, meaning *The Only One*, bestowed upon a Norman knight for outstanding bravery against the native Irish during the Norman conquest of Ireland.

As early settlers, the Uniackes were among the pioneering colonisers, witnesses and participants in the Anglicisation of Ireland. Over the subsequent centuries, many of the English were absorbed into the Gaelic way of life, and their loyalty became suspect in the minds of crown authorities. When the Tudors came to the English throne at the end of the fifteenth century they recognised that Ireland needed to be brought to heel: the Gaelic chieftains were gaining in strength, while the three leading Anglo-Irish lordships – the Butlers of Ormonde, the Fitzgeralds of Kildare and the Fitzgeralds of Desmond – ruled their earldoms as virtual monarchs. English culture and authority remained strong in Dublin and its hinterland, the Pale, and in towns such as Cork, Waterford, Limerick and Youghal.

But Henry VIII's split with the Roman Catholic Church had the most serious impact. He pronounced himself 'Supreme Head' of the Catholic Church in Ireland and initiated the dissolution of the monasteries, which alienated loyal Catholics such as the Uniackes. His daughter, Queen Elizabeth I, introduced further prohibitions on the Catholic religion. Those who did not conform – whether Gaelic or of English extraction – were deemed to be enemies.

The staunchly Catholic Desmonds, determined not to have their local authority usurped by the crown, rebelled against Elizabeth in 1579. They ransacked Youghal before finally being defeated by the Earl of Ormonde. The Desmonds' lands were confiscated and their earldom over much of southern Ireland ended. The Uniackes were connected to the Desmonds by marriage: a James Uniacke was married to Margaret, sister of John FitzEdmond Gerald, the last in a long line of seneschals, who died a prisoner of the crown in 1589. The Uniacke family did not seem to have been penalised by crown authorities for its marriage ties. But it does seem the Uniacke lands and property did not escape the destruction caused by Desmond forces during the rebellion.

When Queen Elizabeth died in 1603 the Uniackes and other Old English Catholic gentry hoped her successor, James I, might be more sympathetic towards them. Indeed, he was more tolerant, as was his son, King Charles I. But the grievances of the Old English were never really addressed – nor indeed could they be. Here was a group of people, English in culture and language, but Catholic in religion, battling against an establishment that saw Roman Catholicism as the arch-enemy of both king and parliament. Their demands for religious freedom could not be conceded. While they were increasingly sidelined politically, the Old English still had considerable economic power in the mid-seventeenth century, holding two-thirds of Irish land.

Immediately after Charles I came to the throne of England in 1625 he embarked on a war against Spain, but he needed the financial support of the Old English. In return, he promised to meet their demands – the granting of their religious freedoms – in an agreement called the Graces. These stubborn Old English recusants were royalists, more than willing to support the king: the king had supremacy in matters temporal, the pope in matters spiritual. Secretly they hoped England could return to the pre-Reformation days. However, Charles' war efforts ended in failure, and with it ended his foreign ambitions; the money spent, the war lost, the king repudiated the Graces. The Old English never succeeded in getting their religious freedoms guaranteed in law.

While they had no control in the Irish parliament in Dublin, the Old English did have some power at local level in certain towns. In the year Charles became king, Maurice Uniacke, who was approximately the same age, was elected a freeman of Youghal. In 1635, he was appointed bailiff, and was elected mayor of Youghal four years later. His religious beliefs were not an obstacle to his holding public office. The people of Youghal were more interested in commerce than religious sectarianism. The town had been a major port since the Middle Ages. Its status was ensured by its location: on the estuary of the river Blackwater, with easy access to the province of Munster and its rich agricultural land. Youghal merchants traded with England, France and Spain. The Uniackes and other rich landed gentry sold their produce in Youghal, much of it for export. With their wealth, they could purchase the fine wines, spices and delicate silks imported from abroad.

In October 1641, the Irish rose up in rebellion, resentful of English dominance. The revolt spread rapidly throughout the country. Anarchy and confusion reigned for the next seven years. The province of Munster was devastated. Rebels besieged Youghal and tried to starve it into surrender. They bombarded the town with cannon, the gunners finding easy targets in the narrow streets of the walled settlement. English ships had to run the gauntlet to get food supplies in. For long stretches the Uniackes had to live off what their burgage plots would provide. They were in constant fear the rebels might take the town and put them to the sword. There were rumours that the Irish were massacring men, women and children.

Many Old English reluctantly joined forces with the rebels, seeing it as the only way to further their interests. But not Maurice Uniacke, he stood by his Protestant neighbours, many of whom had suffered at the hands of the Irish. This must have been a difficult decision, as he ran the risk of excommunication by Rome. Some years later many would testify to his loyalty and 'endeavours for the suppression of the rebels'. But he must have been stung by the English authority's vehemence against all Catholics – accusing them all of disloyalty, barbarism and complicity in the genocide of Protestants. The rebellion produced strong emotions in England. Hatred against popery and the Irish grew. Accounts of atrocities became more embellished on each telling.

However, England was not in a position to avenge these deaths. For many years King Charles I had been at loggerheads with parliament, insisting on his right to raise taxes as he so wished. This was something he took as a Divine Right, bestowed on him by God. But parliament stubbornly resisted attempts to diminish its power and authority. Religion was also fuel on the flames. There was growing popular discontentment with the Church of England among nonconformist Protestants, and with Charles as head of that Church. Worse still, his queen, Princess Henrietta Maria, was a Catholic and became the object of loathing and suspicion. People even said Charles had been seduced by popery. In 1642, the dispute erupted into open conflict and the English Civil War began. The forces of parliament finally defeated the royalists in 1648.

The Uniackes were left impoverished by the years of rebellion and the uncertainty of events in England. Maurice Uniacke died in December 1648. The following month Charles I was beheaded and the last chapter of the English civil war was closed. Parliament could now turn its attention to Ireland.

The Uniacke family managed to retrieve Maurice Uniacke's trunk according to a probate document dated 18 July 1649:

The goods, chattels and credits of Maurice Uniacke, late of Youghal, burgess, deceased, were granted to Margaret Kearney [Margaret Uniacke's maiden name] of Youghal in the county of Cork, widow, during the minority of Thomas Uniacke, son of the said deceased, and executor in his last will and testament named and appointed.

Thomas Uniacke was indeed heir to a substantial estate. The lands of Ballyvergin were on the fertile plateau above Youghal. Its fields and meadows sloped down to the sea and Youghal harbour, with a spectacular view of the White Strand and Capel Island beyond. But his inheritance was a scene of desolation: the large herds of black long-horned cattle that had once grazed the fields were greatly reduced; much of the livestock had been killed or stolen. The crops in the arable fields were frequently torched or trampled on: grain for flour was in short supply, the shortage of fodder meant the animals starved.

Thomas was still a minor at his father's death. His mother was in mourning, and he had several younger siblings to take care of, whose prospects were even paltrier than his. Like his father, Thomas was a devout Catholic, but also an unwavering royalist. Yet, he was powerless to protect his family, carry out his duties as executor of his father's will, defend the Roman Catholic faith and uphold the divine right of the English crown.

The actions of a regicide English parliament angered him. He heard of the successes of a parliamentarian officer called Oliver Cromwell. He was a military genius and a superb cavalry officer – as the achievements at the civil war battles of Marston Moor, Naseby, Preston, Dunbar and Worcester proved. This puritan soldier was violently anti-Catholic and outraged by the atrocities of 'barbarous and bloodthirsty' Irish. In 1649, parliament appointed Cromwell lord lieutenant of Ireland, with the mission to destroy the remaining royalist forces, but above all to crush popery. Cromwell believed God had chosen him for this messianic task. His metaphors were always biblical: he compared his army to the Israelites destroying the idolatrous Canaanites. His men were the instruments of God to overthrow the Empire of Babylon and in its place build the New Jerusalem. The Irish were the barbarous idolaters. And vengeance would be his.

2

Innocent Blood

Over the horizon rose the billowing white sails of some thirty
men-of-war, looming larger and larger like giant ghosts. The ships
glided across the waters of Dublin Bay, the rugged cliffy peninsula of Howth to one side, the forbidding Dublin and Wicklow
mountains stretching away on the other. It was 15 August 1649,
and the fleet of the English parliament led by Oliver Cromwell
had arrived in Ireland. It was bound for the tiny fishing village
of Ringsend at the mouth of the river Liffey, which was then the
port for the city of Dublin. The crossing had been stormy, many
of the soldiers and horses being seasick. As they had waited at
Milton Haven in Wales for conditions clement enough to embark,
they had become unsettled about the approaching campaign.
But their leader, who had distinguished himself so dramatically
in the English Civil War, gave them confidence.

Before long the sleepy community of Ringsend – a settlement of several cabins, a handful of fishing boats and a wooden
quay – was rudely awakened. The fine white sand on that low
spit of land came alive with the noises of an army on the move:
soldiers with their muskets and pikes pouring out of rowing boats;
lines of horses roped together being towed between the ships and
the shore; rafts carrying the huge cannons being heaved towards
the land by rows of soldiers; barrels of gunpowder being rolled
down planks from long boats on to the dry land, the sailors careful not to get them wet; and afterwards the rafts and boats bringing the supplies; finally, vessels with the wives and children who
followed their men throughout the campaign.

The Cromwellian army assembled on the strand of Dublin
Bay was formidable: a 12,000 strong force comprising cavalry,

artillery, pikemen and musketeers. They were called Roundheads because of their closely-cropped hair. Many were experienced, having fought in the major battles of the civil war in England. Cromwell's army had won before – and would again. The cavalry was the crown of the puritan force. The cavalryman wore a steel helmet with a face guard, solid neck guard and cheek pieces. His torso was protected by a breast plate, back plate, and metal elbow gauntlets to protect his upper limbs. The pikeman was muscular and fit, for he had to carry a 16-foot pike in addition to his armour and provisions. He fought in close combat and to protect himself wore a steel pot helmet and breast plate, with tassets to cover the thighs. The musketeer did not wear armour, and was distinguished by his red jacket, a brown, peaked cap called a Montero, grey breeches, blue linen stockings and leather, laced brown shoes. Along with his gun, he carried his bandolier belt strapped across his shoulder carrying the charge boxes and bullet bag. On his back was his knapsack and musket rest.

Fifes and drums played as the soldiers covered the mile or so to Dublin, the fortified capital of English rule in Ireland. Sounds of cannon fire could be heard, as the guns of the city welcomed them. The spirits of the citzens were lifted as they saw Cromwell – the new lord lieutenant of Ireland – leading his army into the city. He was a distinctive figure: riding through the streets on his white horse. Sartorially, Cromwell is recorded as wearing a round, broad-rimmed felt hat, buff waistcoat, grey breeches and black leather boots. He did not stay long in Dublin. By the time he led his army across the river Liffey heading north on 1 September, news had travelled throughout the country of the arrival of this huge force. The country waited anxiously.

Cromwell's destination was Drogheda, a seaport 30 miles north of Dublin. He placed the utmost importance on capturing this medieval walled town, as it was an essential gateway to the north of Ireland, and critical to the security of Dublin. The governor was Sir Arthur Aston, an English Catholic, and a war veteran with a wooden leg. Cromwell was not only in Ireland to quell the natives, but also the remnants of King Charles' army, led by the duke of Ormonde, who was determined to resist the parliamentarian regicides. Ormonde had formed an uneasy alliance with the Irish rebels a few years earlier. In return for their support against the English parliament, greater freedoms had been granted to Catholics. So, incongruously, Aston commanded a force made up of Irish and English troops.

Drogheda had many defensive advantages: a twenty-foot high and six foot thick wall protected it. The town was divided by the river Boyne, the defences encompassing both the northern and southern parts. On the south side, where Cromwell had amassed his troops by 9 September, there were some formidable natural features. This quarter of the town was on a hill, which any army approaching from the south would have to take before it could capture the main town. At the south-east corner was St Mary's church, its high steeple ideal for the defenders to fire upon an attacking army. Along the south wall were the Duleek Gate, which was heavily guarded, and a number of smaller towers. Inside the south wall was the Mill Mount, an artificial hill with a windmill on top, which gave the defenders a complete view of the countryside beyond the walls. Being daring and bold, Cromwell decided to launch the attack from the south-east: if that strategic section were captured, the rest of the town would be his.

Aston had other problems to worry about. Munitions were in short supply and food too would become a problem. The English navy had blockaded the mouth of the river, so no relief could come by sea. Many of his English soldiers were unhappy about fighting their fellow countrymen. The garrison was about 3,000 strong. Aston's artillery force consisted of only one master gunner, two gunners and three gunners' mates. The commander also experienced the treachery of his own grandmother, Lady Wilmot, and several other women of the town. They had been in communication with Colonel Jones and other officers in Cromwell's army. They were hoping that the town might surrender, so avoiding bloodshed. On the evening of 8 September Lady Wilmot had a furious row with her grandson, pleading with him to back down. He would not, and for her disloyalty, that night she was escorted by several cavaliers through the West Gate into the duke of Ormonde's care, who was based at Trim, some fifteen miles inland. Aston was confident: the walls would hold against the enemy cannon; winter was approaching and Cromwell would have to retreat to Dublin.

Cromwell was also conscious of the perils of fighting a winter campaign, so was determined to push ahead. He ordered the cannons to be placed south of the town, facing the Duleek Gate, and to the east, on a hill parallel to the river. Then he penned a letter to Aston:

> Sir,
> Having brought the army belonging to the parliament of England before this place to reduce it to obedience, to the end effusion of blood may be prevented, I thought fit to summon you to deliver the same into my hands to their use. If this be refused, you will have no cause to blame me. I expect your answer and rest,
>
> Your servant,
> O. Cromwell

Having received no reply by mid afternoon Cromwell ordered the white flag that flew over the camp to be replaced by a red ensign. The white flag was apparently a symbol of his intention to settle the siege peacefully if possible. The move put the guards on the walls at the ready. By early evening, the batteries to the south and east began the bombardment, and continued until nightfall.

The barrage resumed at dawn. Cromwell's gunners were up before light in preparation. The first shots of that day were fired from the hill (which came to be called Cromwell's Mount) to the east of the town. Sulphurous white smoke rose from the black barrels as the cannons discharged like a clap of thunder followed by a piercing whistle, the recoil throwing the huge guns backwards. Gunners' mates quickly sponged down the barrels to cool them and extinguish any flames inside. The line of guns fired repeatedly. Wagons carrying cannon balls, barrels of powder and charges were being unloaded at the foot of the hill. The munitions were stacked and passed up by a chain of soldiers as the barrage continued. Captain Edward Tomlins, comptroller of artillery, inspected the operation. He divided his time between the hill and the battery to the south.

By early afternoon, Aston had taken up position on top of the Mill Mount. He saw that the guns were progressively reducing the walls – a breach before day's end was now a real possibility. With each whistle rose a cloud of dust and mortar, as more of the battlements crumbled. The steeple of St Mary's had been demolished, the small gun that had been placed on top destroyed with it. The ideal vantage point for shooting at the attacking army was gone. Aston ordered that retrenchments be built between Duleek Gate and St Mary's in preparation for any breach. By now the corner tower beside the church was missing its outer wall, only the mass of rubble preventing an entry. By mid-afternoon some 400 cannon balls had been fired. Two breaches had been made, on the south and the east. Cromwell called a conference of his senior officers.

Colonel James Castle was ordered to lead his foot regiment through the breaches in the south wall. The attack commenced at five o'clock in the evening. But things did not go to plan. As they scrambled over the rubble and through the holes, they were met by intense musket fire from the retrenchments. Castle's men made it to the trenches and started piking the occupants. Royalist troops were dressed similarly to the parliament's men, except the former wore a red sash, the latter an orange one. The musketmen drew their swords, but were defenceless against sixteen-foot pikes. Within a second, Irish pikemen from the second retrenchment rushed forward to engage the enemy. The defenders put up a ferocious fight. Musket fire was also being directed at the attackers from the walls behind them. Castle was hit in the back of the head and died later. The incident greatly disheartened his men.

A troop of royalist cavalry led by Captain Harpole had joined the fray. These flamboyant horsemen were dressed in plumed felt hats, buff coats, sashes, gauntlets and leather riding boots. The Cromwellians were in a perilous situation. The breaches were too small for the Cromwellian cavalry to enter in any number, depriving their men inside of much needed support. Some musketeers got through the breach and fired upon the royalist cavaliers, managing to hold them back. But the 700 parliamentarian soldiers inside could not hold back Aston's forces for long and made a hasty retreat.

Cromwell was furious when he saw his men running. He took charge of the battle. The lord lieutenant, supported with a fresh reserve of Colonel Ewer's men, galloped towards the walls. But Cromwell's troops were beaten back a second time. Cromwell led his troops in again as the light was waning on that clear September evening. This time they took the trenches.

Cromwell was now effective master of Drogheda. From the Mill Mount, in the failing light, Aston could see how the battle was unfolding. He watched helplessly as his army disintegrated in front of him. Hand to hand fighting was taking place in the graveyard of St Mary's, which Cromwell's troops soon took. The Mill Mount had about 250 soldiers on it, but was nothing more than an island in a sea of blood. The clash of metal on metal rang throughout the town, screams and cries cutting through the air. The assailants were streaming through the two breaches and forcing the defenders back in disarray. They pursued them across the bridge into the northern quarter.

Most of the soldiers on the Mill Mount were either fighting off the attackers or attempting to flee across the river. The governor decided that the only chance of saving any lives was to surrender, though he did not expect fair treatment. Aston stepped from the doorway of the mill to be met by a Lieut Col Axtell and a party of his men. The officer demanded immediate surrender. A mob of Cromwellian soldiers began jostling Aston, because it was rumoured that he kept his gold inside his wooden leg. They tore off the artificial limb only to find the rumour to be false. But searching his jacket and waistcoat they came upon 200 pieces of gold sown into his girdle. They then battered and hacked him to death. Other Irish and royalist officers met the same fate – Sir Edward Verney, Colonels Warren, Fleming, Boyle and Byrne.

The retreating army ran through the narrow streets. A frantic effort was made to close the drawbridge that linked the north and south town, but the parliamentarian forces were too quick and made it across in large numbers. About 100 of Aston's men took refuge in the steeple of St Peter's church. Others occupied towers along the northern walls. Cromwell crossed the Boyne. Arriving at the church, the puritan leader called out to those inside to surrender to the mercy of parliament. A shot rang out. He then ordered the men round him to blast the building by putting barrels of powder in the vaults. But he changed his mind – to preserve his ammunition – and instructed that the pews in the church be stacked beneath the steeple and set alight to burn the occupants. Soldiers clattered into the darkened body of the church with their torches, and in an orderly fashion piled the furniture and ignited it. Screams rose with the flames. Those who tried to escape the inferno were cut down in the church grounds. Only one person survived from the church, by jumping from the top of the steeple. Cromwell rode over to the man and before his soldiers could kill him, spared the man's life: 'I will grant you quarter for the extraordinariness of the thing; to jump such a height you deserve your life'.

An account given by one of Cromwell's young officers, Thomas Wood, showed how innocent women and children suffered. When he was searching the vaults in one of the churches he came upon a group of women and children huddled together. A woman, no more than eighteen, came towards him, tears streaming down her cheeks, head shaking in terror, and pleaded for her life. Out of pity, he lifted her under his arm to carry her out, only to come face to face with one of his comrades. The other plunged his sword into her belly. Wood – seeing her gasping in his arms, a trickle of blood down her chin – dropped her to the ground and snatched her money and jewels.

He also gave a harrowing account of how his fellow soldiers snatched children from houses to use them as shields as they ascended the towers where the enemy was holding out. Watching the indiscriminate massacre from the walls, the remaining soldiers on the defences fired musket rounds down on the parliamentarians, killing several of them. Cromwell could see the flash of the muskets in the dark from near St Peter's. He ordered that the battlements be taken. The officers were to be 'knocked on the head' to a man, every tenth soldier hanged and the rest shipped to Barbados as slaves. The Cromwellians showed no mercy to the religious they found in the city, whether monks administering to the wounded and dying, or those who had taken refuge or had attempted to flee.

The battle within the walls of Drogheda continued for a number of days, until Cromwell's victory was achieved. He afterwards wrote '... this is a righteous judgement of God upon these barbarous wretches, who have imbrued their hands in so much innocent blood'.

The Uniackes followed the news of Cromwell's campaign anxiously, as did everyone else. By the middle of September, reports of a massacre at Drogheda reached them. Further instalments said Cromwell's army was moving south along the east coast. Events were moving fast.

Winter was approaching and Cromwell was determined to follow up on his success at Drogheda. On 1 October, the parliamentarian army encamped outside the walls of Wexford, a crucial port for the enemy in the south-east. Parliament's fleet blocked the town's harbour entrance. Wexford had 2,000 soldiers and about 100 guns around its walls. It also had a number of naval vessels docked in the harbour. Cromwell was so close now that news could travel to Youghal within two days. On 3 October, the Wednesday market day, news arrived of the impending battle. On Friday 12 October, the 'news' of Wexford's fate reached the streets and taverns of Youghal – the fate of Drogheda had been repeated. The stories were told with great tension and flourish. One such account is reconstructed here:

> *Drogheda was not enough for him, every town he passes through must be put to the sword – children, women, the old. Cromwell has massacred the whole population of Wexford but a few score who managed to escape. A friend of mine met one, who hath escaped to Ross, and he brought me the news. It was treachery, a Judas in the town. A soldier called Stafford invited Cromwell's men through. The captain held a castle about 400 paces from the town walls. When the enemy's flag was hoisted up on top of the castle the defenders realised the treachery. The guns of the castle turned down on the walls, the castle being that bit higher – the soldiers fled. As this was happening the gates had been opened for loyal soldiers to get inside. The assailants were too fast and burst forth into the town. The garrison retreated to the market place, where the womenfolk and children were gathered. Cromwell's men killed all stragglers. The heretics even butchered the holy Franciscans. One of the holy men stood on the steps of the church preaching to the townsfolk, while the battle raged around. He even preached to the puritan soldiers, till one ran him through with a sword. The friar fell in a pool of blood, holding his crucifix up to heaven. Hundreds of women and children kneeled before the stone cross in the square and prayed. Cromwell's pikemen impaled them on to the steel points.*

Cromwell had indeed become impatient with the governor of Wexford, Lieut Colonel David Sinnott, who he accused of dragging out negotiations to prolong the battle into winter. Cromwell had refused a truce while the talks continued. He was already losing men to illness, so the batteries continued the cannonade. The actions of Stafford shortened the siege.

Cromwell then turned his attentions to New Ross, a walled town twenty miles west of Wexford, situated on the river Barrow, with a significant facility for seagoing vessels. Sir Lucas Taaffe commanded the town with a force of 1,500 foot soldiers. But Taaffe quickly surrendered and marched out with his troops. Cromwell's army now had winter quarters, and the civilians of New Ross had their lives and property.

Henry Ireton, Cromwell's son-in-law, was sent to attack Duncannon, a fort located on a cliff face overhanging the river Suir, near Waterford city. It was a strategic point in controlling ships destined for Waterford, and its hinterland. Duncannon had three batteries. On the landside, it had a deep ditch and a precipitous rampart. The fort had watchtowers, sally ports and a drawbridge. It would be almost a year before Duncannon would capitulate.

The signals reaching Youghal were confused: on the one hand bloodthirsty accounts of Drogheda and Wexford, on the other a peaceful submission at New Ross and the sparing of its civilian population. This led to a mixture of emotion – fear, panic, claustrophobia, anger, and confusion. Many fled the town: others chose to stay and take their chances. From the evidence, it seems Thomas Uniacke was an impetuous and pugnacious young man. Anecdotal accounts say that he, along with other townsfolk, advocated defending the town against the approaching parliamentarians. If true, these heroics came to nothing and he would have been no match for the Cromwellian army anyway. His bluster about fighting would have more of rage and frustration than reason.

In Youghal much debate centred on whether the English garrison in the town would go over to parliament. The reported atrocities at Drogheda and Wexford persuaded many of the smaller garrisons in the region to surrender. The effective use of artillery was also a factor – medieval walls were no protection against modern technology. In mid October the garrison in Cork declared for parliament. They pillaged the town, driving the Catholic inhabitants out. Swarms of men, women and children staggered into the countryside, into the darkness and pouring rain. Most had only the clothes they wore. Some, barefooted, had only time to grab a blanket or cloak before fleeing.

They brought terrifying accounts with them. At about midnight the population had been woken by cannon fire. They rose immediately and dressed. Then came the sounds of kicking and banging as English soldiers battered in the doors of Catholic homes. The families were driven from the city and warned to hurry, as hunting parties would be out to chase them for sport. Many of the refugees gathered in the fields round Youghal, sheltering in ditches and under hedges. With no room in Youghal, most of them had moved on by evening, taking shelter in the bogs and mountains, in search of places beyond the dark shadow of Cromwell's rule.

The military governor of Youghal, Sir Piercy Smith, along with Colonels Gifford and Warden, decided they would declare for parliament. But another officer who they tried to enlist reported the plot to Lord Inchiquin, the commander of the royalist forces in Munster, who was based at Castlelyons, some miles away. He quickly dispatched a troop of cavalry to surround the town. Inchiquin's decisiveness meant there had been no time to call for support from Cromwell. Smith seized a number of royalists and tried to negotiate terms to end the stand off. The bartering went on for a tense day across the town walls. Few people ventured from their homes. Smith demanded indemnity, to which Inchiquin agreed, possibly because he did not want open war among his own soldiers. Smith remained as governor, now having thrown in his lot with the royalists and the Irish. Youghal settled back into an uneasy peace.

Later, rumours began circulating that Inchiquin was going to place an Irish garrison in Youghal, enraging the English garrison there and unsettling the Protestant inhabitants. In early November, a Captain Henry Smithwick discussed this with his fellow officer, Captain John Widenham. They wanted the town to revolt and go over to parliament. If an Irish garrison were based in Youghal, they would have a bloody fight on their hands. It was agreed that Widenham would go to Cork for help.

On 7 November, he returned with a troop of cavalry, arriving at the South Gate at about seven o'clock in the evening. Sir Piercy Smith got word from a scout that they were coming, but there was insufficient time to close the gate. That gate led into Friar Street, up to another gate between two towers, called the Trinity Gate. The governor just had time to order that the chain be drawn across this gate. The horsemen stopped at the entrance. Colonel Gifford, who was commanding the soldiers, ordered the gate to be opened and the officer of the guard be summoned. A sergeant standing by the gate ran to the White Hart where Ensign Dashwood and town-major Smith were drinking and having a meal. They rushed to the gate. Dashwood ignored the governor's command to stand back. He called for Widenham through the portcullis. Widenham replied, and said they had come on the orders of parliament. The ordinary soldiers were relieved when Dashwood then told them to remove the chains and open the iron gate. Sir Piercy roared that they must not open until the 'terms of surrender have been negotiated', but was once again ignored. Realising the hopelessness of his position he ran back up the street to his residence on North Main Street.

Near midnight Colonel Gifford and Captain Widenham met the Mayor of Youghal, Thomas Warren, in the mayoral chambers of the corporation's meeting hall, the tholsel. Also at the meeting were the town recorder, Joshua Boyle, and Thomas Taylor. Warren wrote the following letter to the lord lieutenant, Oliver Cromwell:

May it please your excellency we have a long time been humble suitors of Almighty God for that happy success of your endeavours. Our humble suit to you is that we may possess your honour's favour in protection of our charter, privilege, lives and estates.

Youghal was now politically and militarily in the hands of Cromwell. The aldermen of the town had submitted, the garrison had switched and its governor was a prisoner. They awaited a response. Three days later, the naval frigate, *Nonsuch*, dropped anchor outside the harbour. A boat was sent ashore for the mayor, who in the gold chain and crimson velvet gown, went out to meet Cromwell's representative. On board was Lord Broghill, one of parliament's leading generals. He was the third son of the earl of Cork. He was a devout Protestant, and – as his father had – detested Catholicism. Thomas Warren tried to find out from Broghill what conditions the corporation should seek from parliament. Broghill bluntly warned him that it 'would be more for their honour and advantage to desire no conditions.' The mayor promptly demurred.

Even though Duncannon still held out Cromwell was heartened by the revolts of Cork and Youghal. Cromwell had also besieged Waterford, a staunchly Catholic city that was well defended and had ample supplies. He knew he was not in a strong position to capture these two remaining towns on the south coast, but he had achieved an enormous amount: the enemies of parliament were in tatters. But God's work had still to be done.

As the war progressed into early December, it became obvious that the armies would have to suspend hostilities until the spring. The mildness of the winter had allowed Cromwell prolong his campaign. But by then the parliamentarian army had been reduced to about 3,000 troops. The rest were either dead or incapacitated by 'country sickness', probably a form of dysentery caused by the unsanitary conditions of the camps. Cromwell himself had a fever.

On 2 December, he had recovered sufficiently to lead the remains of his army away from Waterford towards Dungarvan on the coast. The news preceded him – so did rumours of atrocities. Butlerstown Castle outside the liberties of Waterford was the first casualty, being seized and blown up. Kilmeaden by the river Suir was destroyed. It belonged to the Le Poers, an ancient Anglo-Irish family, landowners in Co. Waterford for centuries. It was reported that one of the Le Poer family was taken out and hanged from a nearby tree. A daughter locked her father – a staunch royalist – in the dungeon of his own home at Curraghmore as the parliamentarians approached. Cromwell himself is said to have come to the door of the castle. When the daughter dutifully answered the knock, she protested her father's unflinching support for the English state. The castle and the estate were spared. Dunhill Castle, just east of Dungarvan, was not so fortunate; it was blown up with its occupants in it.

When Cromwell's army reached Dungarvan on 4 December these latest stories had filtered through to the taverns, the marketplace and back lanes of Youghal. A day or two later conflicting accounts of Dungarvan's fate began circulating – one saying that the entire population had been massacred as at Drogheda and Wexford. But this proved to be apocryphal. Quickly a story spread that the lives of the townsfolk had been saved by the actions of a woman called Nagle. Cromwell had intended to kill everyone, but as he rode through the town at the head of his troops and they were just about to carry out his order, she ran out in front of him. She held up a flagon of beer and drank to his good health, offering him the flagon. The general was impressed by her courage and courtesy and accepted her offer. He then told his soldiers to partake of the drink, which the woman's servants supplied in abundance. So, Dungarvan was saved. This story produced some sense of nervous relief among the Catholics and royalists of Youghal. Next day Cromwell continued his march west.

It was not long before the first dragoons arrived at Ferrypoint, a flat sandy spit on the east bank of the river Blackwater, facing Youghal. News of their approach travelled fast. Yet the sight of the roundheads was terrifying. Then the faint sounds of the fife and drum were heard – getting nearer and nearer – rippling across the waters of the estuary. Columns of pikes rising over the hedgerows could be seen as the bulk of the army marched along the Dungarvan road towards Ferrypoint. The musketeers were distinctive in their red coats.

However the Cromwellian army looked more dejected than victorious as it assembled in the long narrow main street of Youghal. Soldiers and horses stood round at every corner, the sick lay in wagons, groaning and shivering. The four months of campaign had taken its toll. The musketeers' red jackets were muddied and wet, their breeches and blue stockings torn. Some were desperately in need of footwear, their brown leather shoes in tatters having marched for hundreds of miles. Even the fine cavalrymen were dejected, their horses weak and thin. Pikes stood against the walls of buildings, their muscular carriers glad of the rest. Many had even cut the ends of their pikes to make them shorter and lighter to carry. Some of the pikemen had discarded their armour and pot helmets in the wagons. They had campaigned long enough for one season: Cromwell made Youghal his winter quarters. The soldiers were billeted in the homes of the townsfolk and in the areas surrounding. Many homes had been deserted as inhabitants fled the approaching army.

Inevitably, the presence of large numbers of soldiers brought trouble. Locals were terrorised, a common feature of wars in Ireland: the troops treated their 'hosts' in an arrogant fashion, plundering and pilfering when it suited them. When Cromwell heard this, he immediately issued a proclamation, to warn his troops and reassure the citizens of Youghal:

> *Whereas I am informed that the horse under my command (since their being quartered within the Blackwater) have and do in their*

several quarters take away and waste wheat and barley for their horses, and do behave themselves outrageously towards the inhabitants, not contenting themselves with such provisions as they are able to afford them, but do kill their sheep and other cattle within and as often as they please.

I do hereby straight charge and command all soldiers to forebear such like practices upon pain of death. And I do further will and require all officers and soldiery within the limits aforesaid, that they do not break down any stacks of barley or wheat in their respective quarters, to give the same to their horses; but that they content themselves with peas, oats, hay and such other forage, as the country affords, paying or giving tickets at such reasonable rates for the same as they were usually sold for, before their coming into the said quarters.

The proclamation had a dramatic effect. The strategy adopted by Cromwell was a shrewd one. Troops were forbidden to pillage and destroy. The peasants and farmers were encouraged to sell their produce to the army. The soldiers knew the penalty for disobeying this order: they remembered that grim spectacle on the road to Drogheda, when two of their fellow soldiers were hanged by the side of the road for stealing chickens from a poor peasant woman. There was good reason for this policy: the army would not alienate the local population and would not be dependent on food supplies from Dublin, which could be interrupted by enemy attack. In the rules of the Cromwellian army stealing from natives carried the death penalty, as did treason, murder and rape. Cromwell knew soldiers were an unruly crowd but he would not accept indiscipline, lewdness and drunkenness.

With the army came typhus, or spotted fever, spread by the micro-organism, Rickettsia Prowazeki. Within weeks many soldiers and townsfolk died. The disease spread like wildfire. It is not known if the Uniacke family was affected, but the 'plague' hung over everyone's head like a Sword of Damocles. The seventeenth-century physicians had no effective treatment, and no idea it was spread by lice, which ingested the blood of an infected person, then deposited infected faeces on to another person in close proximity. Oblivious, the individual would scratch the skin, infecting the blood. In the streets or market an otherwise innocuous cough could be the first sign. Other symptoms were severe headache, pains in the back and limbs. But only the early stages were witnessed by the public eye. Feeling the onset of a flu-type illness the person sought their bed. There, the despairing and helpless family could only watch: the patient developed a high fever, became confused and delirious – twisting and turning and threshing about, rambling and unable to recognise anyone. As the heartbeat became fainter, the battle was being lost. Death could be caused by a number of side effects: septicaemia, heart or kidney failure, or pneumonia.

During the day the town was almost empty. People only ventured out if they really had to. The sound of commerce was replaced by the scraping of shovels as fresh graves were dug in the cemetery. St Mary's was not far from the Uniacke home. It could be glimpsed from the left-hand corner of an upstairs window: a sea of grey and white headstones perched on the top of the hill. But there was also another sound, the clanking of metal, as soldiers removed the copper bells from the belfry. The bells were lowered onto wagons and taken to Cork, where they were melted down to make cannon balls.

Cromwell's presence in Youghal brought fear and intrigue – but also excitement, especially for children. Every morning at nine o'clock the troops assembled on North Main Street to be inspected. A line three-deep would stretch from Trinity Gate to North Gate. Then the little man with his rough warty face appeared from the low mullioned doorway of a house on the street which had been made into his headquarters. Ironically, the building had once belonged to Benedictine monks.

The children heard horrible tales about this man. The daily routine was carried out not far from the Uniacke household, and it attracted the attention of the Uniacke children, especially eight-year-old James.

In the midst of disease and death came a piece of macabre pageantry, the funeral of Lieut General Jones, one of Cromwell's most senior officers. He died in Dungarvan of fever and was brought to Youghal for burial. The body was carried along the coast road to Ferrypoint, on the eastern shore of Youghal Bay, then by boat across the estuary to the town. It was a dark December evening, and the spectacle was an eerie sight for the locals. The gun carriage with the draped body made its way under the tight Water Arch that led from the quays, up the dark narrow lane to Trinity Gate and the main street and on towards St Mary's collegiate church at the top of Church Street.

St Mary's stood behind a wrought iron pillared gateway. The church was a desolate place, on the steep slope nestled beneath the north-west corner of the town walls, surrounded by slanted and weather-beaten gravestones and tombs. The chancel was roofless. The belfry was an old medieval tower built in earlier centuries to defend the settlers against the native Irish.

The torch-lit funeral procession gathered in the south transept under the impressive tomb built by the earl of Cork. Before the body was interred in the vaults Cromwell gave a moving oration to the gathered congregation of soldiers and town citizens. He praised his comrade's valour, honour and fidelity, and described how Jones had been loved and respected by his troops.

Later rumours suggested that Cromwell had poisoned Jones, who was believed to have disapproved of the king's execution. He may also have been jealous that the English parliament had made Cromwell supreme commander of the Irish campaign, and not himself. A few months before Cromwell's arrival in Ireland, Jones defeated the royalist army at Rathmines, now a suburb of Dublin. This effectively gave Cromwell the bridgehead to land his forces. Lord Broghill later claimed that Jones summoned him to his deathbed. Denouncing Cromwell, Jones begged Broghill to overthrow the lord lieutenant of Ireland. Nothing was done.

On Christmas morning, the people of Youghal were woken

by the trumpet call as the troops were mustered for their daily inspection. Christmas day was no exception for the puritan preachers who accompanied the army. They reviled festive frivolity that they considered profanity and debauchery. Christmas was an occasion for prayer, reflection and sober living. The preachers would not allow the occasion of Christ's birth to be used as an excuse for immoral ways.

For the Uniackes it was the second Christmas Margaret was without her husband, Maurice, and the children, their father. Furthermore, the land was gripped by disease, trade had slumped and the big market held in mid December had been a meagre affair. The future was uncertain: in spring, crops would have to be planted for the following autumn and winter. And because of the rain, the coming spring harvest would probably be poor.

The religious preparations for Christmas normally started in Advent, but under puritan rule any such devotions had to be private. Devout Catholic families like the Uniackes would add additional prayers to their morning and evening devotions. Children were urged to say paters and aves. A few days before Christmas holly, ivy, bay and other evergreens were collected and brought home to decorate the house. The children helped to make a cross out of sticks tied around with sprigs of holly. Holly with berries was particularly prized for these decorations. The greenery was collected from the scrubland and woodlands on the estate. The family also visited the tenants and despite the straitened times, gave presents of meat, eggs, butter and milk. There were far fewer tenants than the previous year; large numbers had fled as Cromwell approached. They had not returned and the winter weather was getting worse. Either they had perished in the wilderness or found refuge in parts of the country out of parliament's control.

Traditionally Christmas Eve was a day of fast, a meal of fish being eaten in the evening. Many households lit a candle in the principal window of the home at dusk. Sometimes three candles were lit, representing the Holy Trinity. Christmas dinner was usually either beef or fowl, supplemented with cakes, puddings, pies, apples and dried fruit. For the wealthy, there were Spanish and French wines to drink with the meal and Madeira to sip afterwards. But that Christmas of 1649, the future looked impoverished.

For Catholics, Cromwell's sweeping successes created a political and religious vacuum. This was somewhat filled by the pamphlet issued by the Irish hierarchy which met in December at Clonmacnoise, on the eastern bank of the river Shannon.

> *By the ecclesiastical congregation of the kingdom of Ireland, we, the archbishops and other ordinaries and prelates of the kingdom of Ireland, having met at Clonmacnoise proprio motu on the 4th day of December in the year of our Lord God 1649, taking into our consideration among others the affair then agitated and determined for the preservation of the kingdom, that many of our flock are misled with a vain opinion of hopes that the commander-in-chief of the rebel forces, commonly called parliamentarians, would afford them good conditions, and that relying thereon, they suffer utter destruction of religion, lives and fortunes, if not prevented. To undeceive them in this their ungrounded expectation, we do thereby declare as a most certain truth that the enemy's resolution is to extirpate the Catholic religion out all his majesty's dominions, as by their several covenants doth appear, and the practice wherever their power doth extend ...*

It stated that estates would be confiscated, and both lord and tenant banished.

> *And in effect this banishment and other destruction of the common people must follow the resolution of extirpating the Catholic religion, which is not to be effected without the massacring or banishment of the Catholic inhabitants.*

The pamphlet warned the population not to be deluded and called on 'the gentry and inhabitants, for God's glory and their own safety to the utmost of their power to contribute with patience to the support of the war against that enemy in the hope that with the blessing of God they may be rescued from the threatened evils ... '

About a week later, the hierarchy issued a second proclamation. It called for unity behind King Charles II and decreed that:

> ... All the archbishops, and other ordinaries, within their respective dioceses shall enjoin public prayers, fasting, general confessions, and receiving, and other works of piety, toties quoties, to withdraw from this nation God's anger and to render capable of his mercies.
>
> ... All the pastors and preachers be enjoined to preach unity. And for inducing the people thereunto, to declare unto them the absolute necessity that is for the same, and as the chief means to preserve the nation against extirpation and destruction of their religion and fortunes resolved on by the enemy.
>
> Divisions between provinces or families, or between old English and old Irish, or any English or Scot adhering to his majesty.
>
> Any clergy fomenting such dissension or unnatural divisions be punished by their respective prelates and superiors.

It warned that those creating division – lay or religious – would 'answer to God for the evils that thereout may ensue'.

The Uniackes, like other Catholics in Youghal, could do little to support the campaign against the puritans. The community was crippled, Cromwellian soldiers kept a careful scrutiny of everything and everybody. Cromwell started to plan his strategy for the spring campaign after Christmas. Once the weather and his troops were well enough he would forge ahead, with that impatient yet methodical determination that always brought him victory.

Before he left Youghal, Cromwell composed a document in response to statements published by the Irish Catholic bishops the previous month. And he replied at length and with some vitriol:

> Your covenant is with death and hell; your union is like that of Simeon and Levi. Associate yourself, and you shall be broken in

pieces; take counsel together, and it shall come to naught. For though it becomes us to be humble in respect of ourselves, yet we can say to you, God is not with you ... You forewarn the people of their danger; which you make to consist: first, in the extirpation of the Catholic religion; secondly, in the destruction of their lives; thirdly, in the ruin of their fortunes ... I shall not, where I have power, and the Lord is pleased to bless me, suffer the excise of the Mass, where I find you seducing the people, or by an overt act violating the laws established; but if you come in my hands, I shall cause to be inflicted the punishments appointed by the law ...

On the accusation that the population would be massacred or banished he replied:

I shall not willingly take or suffer to be taken away the life of any man not in arms, but by the trial to which the people of this nation are subject by law, for offences against the same. And for the banishment, it hath not hitherto been inflicted on any but such who, being in arms, upon the terms they were taken might justly have been put to death – as those instanced in the Declaration to be sent to the Tobacco Islands. And therefore I do declare, that if the people be ready to run to arms by the instigation of their clergy or otherwise, such as God by His providence shall give into my hands may expect that or worse measure from me, but not otherwise ...

... For such of the nobility, gentry and commons of Ireland as have not been actors in this rebellion, they shall and may expect the protection in their goods, liberties and lives which the law gives them. They behaving themselves as becomes honest and peaceable men, testifying their good affections, upon all occasions, to the service of the State of England, equal justice shall be done them with the English. They shall bear proportionably with them in taxes. And if the soldiery is insolent upon them, upon complaint and proof, it shall be punished with utmost severity, and they protected equally with Englishmen.

And having said this, and purposing honestly to perform it, if this people shall headily run on after the counsels of their Prelates and Clergy and other leaders, I hope to be free from the misery and desolation, blood and ruin, that shall befall them, and shall rejoice to exercise utmost severity against them.

On the morning of 29 January 1650, the army assembled as usual. With fifes and drums playing, Cromwell led his troops out of Youghal. The town could once again return to civilian life. The Uniackes had survived.

The shadow of death had moved on – but worse was yet to come.

3

War ... Plague ... and Famine

Cromwell's march brought him through north Co. Cork, along the southern banks of the river Blackwater to the town of Mallow. From Cork, he moved into Co. Tipperary. Cromwell was spellbound by the beauty of the landscape. Some years later he was granted large estates in the area. It is said he stood on a hill overlooking the Golden Vale and commented: 'This, indeed, is a country worth fighting for'.

Once again, any resistance was overcome. The town of Fethard received exceptionally favourable terms for surrender, suggesting Cromwell was anxious for a speedy conclusion to the siege. His army reached the town after dark and set up camp in an old abbey outside the walls. A trumpeter was sent to the gate, carrying a message to surrender. A musket shot was fired at him and he hastily retreated. But later that night, the governor sent out two officers to negotiate. By six o'clock the following morning terms had been agreed. The prompt capitulation of Fethard had saved all civilian inhabitants from plunder and death – even the Catholic clergy were spared.

The garrison at Cashel fled once it heard of the advancing army. The town aldermen quickly sued for peace, and Cromwell accepted their submission. In the heart of north Tipperary, Cashel became the headquarters for this phase of his Irish campaign. Located on the fertile plains, the town nestles in the shadow of the Rock of Cashel, upon which stands a great complex of monastic churches and towers, the high point of native Irish and Romanesque architecture in Ireland. Before basing himself in Cashel, Cromwell besieged Cahir about ten miles south. Cahir Castle had high walls, a strong gate and a drawbridge. Here the parliamentarians met with their first stiff resistance since leaving Youghal. The garrison was well supplied. Cromwell's soldiers attempted to scale the courtyard walls but were beaten back. Finally, the devastating effect of artillery forced the besieged to seek quarter. As at other battles the garrison marched out, flags flying and drums beating.

On 19 March, Cromwell met up with Colonel Hewson, who had been moving south through the country from his base in Dublin. Three days later, the combined forces were before Kilkenny, the ancient medieval city that boasted an impressive twelfth-century castle overlooking the river Nore. It was home to the Butlers of Ormonde, one of the most powerful Anglo-Norman families in Ireland. James Butler, duke of Ormonde, commanded the royalist forces in the country. Kilkenny was also the seat of the Irish Confederacy, the provisional Irish parliament formed in 1642. The garrison was under the command of one of the duke's cousins, Sir Walter Butler. In addition to being besieged, Kilkenny was also in the grip of the bubonic plague, which is believed to have reached Ireland via a Spanish ship landing in Galway on the western seaboard.

At one point Cromwell faced a mutiny, so demoralised were his men. Ormonde's troops were allowed to leave, but had to give up their weapons two miles down the road. Priests also were left unmolested. While the townsfolk were assured of safety, they had to pay parliament £2,000 for the privilege – and the soldiers went on an orgy of vandalism. Any symbols of Catholicism were profaned: crosses, vestments, books and holy paintings were burned in the street. Soldiers used the market cross for target practice. The Ormonde family tomb in St Canice's Cathedral was desecrated, and the cathedral was used as a stable. The duke of Ormonde retreated further inland, severely shaken by the news of Kilkenny's fall. He needed a plan of action if Cromwell was to be pushed back.

By spring the plague – sweeping through the island – had

reached Youghal. News of the pestilence spread, each market day bringing more instalments of its virulent progress. The tightly confined marketplace along the main street, the taverns and the stalls, were the ideal location for the dissipation of both news and plague. The disease, *Yersinia pestis*, was carried by the fleas of the black rat, living in the rodent's fur and when the infected vermin died the insect leapt from the carcass in search of a new source of blood.

People had to eat and live – and make a profit – so life went on. Servants brought vegetables and other produce from the burgages. Herdsmen channelled long-horned black cattle through the narrow street. Milkmaids rode on the back of carts with churns of milk and butter. The town bustled with buyers and sellers. The poorer people were the first to arrive at the stalls, as under corporation by-laws the poor of the town and liberties were served before the more prosperous inhabitants. The clerk helped buyers and sellers of corn measure their produce in the market house. He had an important job, determining the trading price so the mayor could set the price of bread for the following week. Every type of item was for sale. Each trader shouted out the great value of his or her wares. As well as stalls selling farm produce, there were butchers, victuallers, shoemakers, gloviers, alemakers and clothmakers. Horse traders kept up a boisterous trade as purchasers pushed and jostled to outbid each other, while the keeper of the tolls tried desperately to get the details of the person who finally bought an animal.

As usual, arguments arose. The street was so narrow many of the pitches ended up blocking the doors to houses, causing a lot of friction between trader and householder and if the entrance was blocked, 1d had to be paid to the dweller. Pitches could not be more than eight inches over the channel, a constant cause of dispute with market officials. Buyers haggled and complained with butchers over the quality of meat, and tested the hides of animals to make sure the animal had not been stolen. Butchers had to bring the hides to market to verify such points. Street cleaners fought an uphill battle to keep the ground clean. The channels became covered in dung, discarded vegetables and fruit, pieces of meat, hides, tallow and cloth. The cleaners had to roar at children running between the crowds, or swipe at a roaming pig or chicken.

The humdrum of everyday commercial life carried on despite war and upheaval. The Uniackes arranged that the town bailiff got his 2d for the marketplace. As the terrible pestilence became reality the numbers coming to market began to dwindle. On each market day – Wednesday and Saturday – the crowds got thinner and the silence more eerie.

As people mingled, fleas moved easily from rats to the clothes and hair of humans. In their fear and dread most would not even have noticed the tiny pinprick nip on the skin and the reddened itch that followed. The deadly flea, called *Xenopsylla cheopis*, inflicted symptoms no different to the *Pulex irritans*, the human flea. The victims sought other portents and signs to explain the coming of the pestilence. People interpreted the world in terms of punishment, penance and superstition and relied on unscientific treatments, putting faith in unproved herbs and potions.

The first symptoms could be a range of infections – fever, shivering and headaches. These could be the plague or something quite innocuous. But if these were followed by buboes, the victim had been afflicted, and would most likely die. The signs appeared usually on the groin, less frequently under the armpits, and guaranteed almost certain death. The 'patient' often had seizures, and would writhe in agony, desperate for water, the skin like a hot poker. The person would drift in and out of consciousness. Often the buboes would burst, releasing a black liquid that gave off a revolting stench.

Eventually the town was deserted and the market closed as the weeks passed. Those who could leave had already done so.

In reality few must have left, as there was nowhere to go. The country was in the grip of war. The gates of Youghal were shut, to keep inhabitants in and travellers out. For many the town would be their coffin. The quay became silent, no ships arrived, no cargoes were unloaded, and no merchandise was brought to the harbour for export. The entire town was deserted: along Friar Street in the south end of the town, through the Trinity Gate, up Main Street, past the market cross and the side streets and lanes – all was silent. No one left their homes unless they were able to, or had to. The bustle of this important town had vanished. The noises that replaced it were the groans and coughs of people locked in their homes, as their conditions worsened, left to either recover or die. Houses that fell quiet would start releasing the stench of rotting flesh as the days went on.

The authorities in Youghal attempted to control the spread of disease. Once the doctor diagnosed the condition, the patient was quarantined. Victims were confined to their homes, the windows and doors boarded, leaving them in the gloom with only chinks of light filtering through from the outside. A red cross was daubed on the front door, often with the words 'Lord Have Mercy Upon Us' written beside it. Wardens were employed to ensure the infected did not leave their homes, and any nurse attending the sick could not leave for some weeks after the victim died. Officials were appointed to check if victims were dead. But often the stench of rotting flesh would tell them. Some attempts were made to sterilise the houses where individuals – frequently whole families – had perished. Bedding had to be aired by a fire and perfumed before being used again. People, even in those chaotic times, were responsible for sweeping the front of their houses and removing rubbish.

The Uniacke family, while perhaps physically unaffected, carried other scars of the trauma. From their home on the main street, they witnessed the comings and goings of carts carrying the dead neighbours to the graveyard in St Mary's. From a window overlooking the street, they could see the corporation workers, handkerchiefs covering their faces, tossing corpses into the wagons. With a lash of a whip, the workers would resume their solemn journey, probably led by a preacher. The bodies were generally removed just before dawn or after sunset. From the cemetery came the monotonous sound of shovelling, as the gravediggers excavated mass pits to accommodate the seemingly endless train of burials. But as the months went on the numbers of new cases began to lessen. The hammering of houses being boarded up, the shrieking and wailing of the bereaved, the rumble of carts, the ploughing of the cemetery earth ceased. The townsfolk returned to their normal life as best they could, children began to play on the streets. Once again, people got on with their lives.

By the end of April 1650, Cromwell was starting his final battle on Irish soil. At Clonmel, he came up against the military skills of Hugh O'Neill, of the once-great Ulster Gaelic dynasty, the grandnephew of the Hugh O'Neill who had fought the Nine Years War against Queen Elizabeth I. Young Hugh was the nephew of Colonel Owen Roe O'Neill, who had returned from the continent in the 1640s, where he had been an officer in the Spanish army. Unfortunately, this respected military leader had died in November 1649, before getting a chance to pit his forces against Cromwell's. The O'Neills wanted the removal of all English authority in Ireland, so were detested by Old English Catholics such as the Uniackes. O'Neill had 1,500 Ulster Irish troops in Clonmel. The town was short of ammunition and supplies. But what the Irish soldier lacked in munitions he made up for in initiative. Cromwell's cannon had made a number of breaches in the walls, so O'Neill set the garrison and citizens to work: using stone, timber, dung, mortar they constructed long lanes leading inwards from the breaches. These lanes were about six feet high and eighty yards in length. When the English forces entered the breaches, they were funnelled down narrow channels – straight into cannon and musket fire. They retreated. Meanwhile, Cromwell was waiting at the gates of the town, expecting his men attacking the breach to open them at any minute. But to his dismay, he saw the soldiers pouring back out of the breaches. He sent in his cavalry, who were also repulsed. The situation was looking grave: Cromwell feared that his army could be beaten by a sally from the garrison. In the battle for Clonmel, 2,000 Cromwellian soldiers are believed to have died.

O'Neill, knowing it was only a matter of time before his enemies took the town, slipped out with his troops in the middle of the night. Before going, he advised the mayor to make peace with the forces of parliament. Terms were agreed, and Cromwell entered on 10 May. But he was furious to discover that O'Neill had escaped. When he confronted the mayor on why he had not told him of this, the mayor replied that Cromwell had never asked. Cromwell did not break the agreement, but swore he would pursue O'Neill and destroy him. But the lord lieutenant's time in Ireland was near its end. He was required in Westminster by parliament. The pursuit of O'Neill would have to be left to others. He left his son-in-law Henry Ireton in command.

On 16 May, a naval ship, *The President*, was docked along the quay in Youghal. Later that day it took Cromwell back to Bristol. On that sunny morning, Cromwell witnessed a desolate scene as he emerged from the gates of the Boyle residence where he had stayed the night. He led his cavalcade through the streets of a near-empty town, stripped bare by months of war and bubonic plague, down the narrow lane that led to the harbour.

Famine was now competing with the plague for victims. Both armies had pursued a scorched earth policy, torching vast areas of crops. No new crops had been planted that spring. Autumn loomed and there was no grain for baking bread nor fodder to see surviving livestock through the winter. Cows became weak and thin, milk yields fell. When one would die, ravenous peasants that roamed the countryside would swarm round the carcass like flies, cutting away what little flesh there was. Horrific tales of cannibalism circulated: how entire families would drag a passer-by from his horse, strip him, roast him on a spit in their cabin, and eat him down to the very bone, afterwards concealing the bones in shallow graves. Such tales were probably apocryphal, but the true picture of famine was every bit as horrendous.

War drove the poor off their meagre pieces of land. With no livestock or crops, they had neither income nor food. The countryside was moving closer to starvation. Children cried and fretted for food. They succumbed to hunger and cold faster than adults, the younger the more vulnerable. They grew increasingly weak from the lack of milk; finally fever and dehydration killed them. The weak and the dying often became meals for the pack of ravenous wolves that roamed the land. Where parents had the strength, a child was buried close to the cabin. When older people died, where they fell became their grave. Some might crawl to the shelter of a hedgerow, or come to die in a piece of isolated woodland, their corpses to rot away anonymously. Others chose to end their lives in their cabins. A door swinging on its hinge was the only welcoming sound to the lonely traveller on those desolate country roads.

Others fled to the towns and areas less affected. Great multitudes arrived at the gates of Youghal. They staggered along the roads, passed the corpses of others who had died before them, struggling to make it to a place where they could get food and water. They groaned with the hunger pains, and begged for help. Many had green stains round their mouths from trying to eat grass and weeds. Babies tried to suckle from empty sagging breasts. Parents, who had made their children trek for days in the hope of food, now had to watch them die. Their bodies went from lean to gaunt and their legs became spindly. Their cadaverous skin shrivelled, and their ribs showed through their torsos. But even after such a pilgrimage, there was no salvation. There was no food to spare for such a multitude. Many of the victims died from famine-induced dysentery and other diseases. The population became weakened by inadequate diet or eating unsuitable food, such as seashells, which were difficult to cook properly.

The Uniacke family had food from the burgage plots and a small income from what the land could produce, though their rental income had been decimated. They were not starving but they knew that even their relatively secure state could worsen: rumours were rife that all Catholics were to be killed or at least driven off the land, to seek their food and shelter in the bogs and mountains. A new, bold plantation would replace them all with English Protestants.

Young men like Thomas Uniacke found oblivion at the White Hart and other taverns in Youghal. Beer was becoming scarce and expensive. But at least the drinkers could take hope from the strange tales of supposedly supernatural intervention, how Cromwellian soldiers died hideously – as divine punishment. These stories were told with great flourish. Since setting foot in Ireland 'the abominable heretics' fell victims to the most bizarre happenings. One parliamentarian soldier got the blood of his victim on his hand. He tried to wash it off, but was unable to. He carried the mark for all to see. The soldier himself related the story to Mr John French. Another tried to shoot a monk that lay wounded, but the bullet just rolled off the cowl; he tried again, the same happened. Refusing to fire a third time, he said: 'I have done so already as well as I could.'

The worst punishment fell on those who blasphemed the Catholic faith: some of the soldiers put on the habits of monks they'd killed, out of mockery. That night one soldier had nightmares that mad dogs were dragging him about. So horrific was the spectre that the man took ill and died. Another dropped to the ground while uttering blasphemies, and died.

Fr Raymond Stafford was one of the Franciscans who stood with his flock as they were being massacred in the marketplace. A musket round hit the crucifix he was holding, ricocheted, and struck an officer right in the heart. At the same time as the killings were taking place Fr John Turner was travelling five miles outside Wexford when he saw a vision, a beautiful woman ascending into the sky. Fr Turner had no knowledge of the bloodbath happening until later that day. A company of soldiers was quartered in the convent that had belonged to the religious order. Many died mysteriously, their bodies buried in the convent cemetery. Others were so haunted by nightmares they would stay no longer in the place, preferring to sleep out of doors, in the woods or on the streets of the town. In Kilkenny, six soldiers dropped dead shortly after they had desecrated the market cross in the centre of the city.

Henry Ireton would pursue his father-in-law's campaign in Ireland until 1652, when all meaningful opposition had been crushed. By the end of 1650 parliament controlled the whole country east of the river Shannon. The city of Limerick, on the banks of that river, surrendered on 27 October 1651. Hugh O'Neill, who had retreated there after Clonmel, was taken prisoner and brought over to London. There he was jailed, until after several months Spanish diplomatic efforts won his release. Galway was the last city to surrender. The port city on the Atlantic shores accepted the inevitable on 12 April 1652. Many of the soldiers – and priests – were allowed to leave the country. Some 30,000 soldiers left Ireland to become mercenaries in continental armies. Ormonde had left the country in late 1650 and any hope of reversing events was gone. He joined Charles II in France.

All resistance in Ireland had been stamped out. The puritan English parliament could now start implementing its laws and policies to eradicate organised Catholicism in Ireland.

4

Unsettling of a Nation ...

The aim of the Cromwellian land settlement was to replace Irish Catholics, and their English co-religionists, with loyal Protestant settlers. The Catholic population was transplanted *en masse* to Connaught, a province in the west of the island. There they would eke out an existence on the rocky infertile soil of that barren but beautiful terrain. Cut off by the Atlantic Ocean on one side and the river Shannon on the other, it was a natural prison. A line of defences along the east bank was to be constructed, a bulwark against marauding rebels. The Protestant settlers in Ireland would be secure and safe.

The English parliament had debts to honour. During the 1640s, England had needed to raise funds for its campaign against the Irish. In 1642, it introduced the Adventurers' Act, whereby businessmen financed the war: in return, they would be given lands in Ireland. Furthermore, by 1653 there were some 30,000 parliamentarian soldiers garrisoned in the country. Payments to these were already in arrears and the solution was to give them land in lieu of money. To meet the various demands upon it, parliament brought in the Act of Settlement in September 1653. The new law finally became a reality in late 1653 when a notice was nailed on to the door of the tholsel in Youghal. The order to transplant had come. The list contained the names of Catholic gentry and merchants long associated with Youghal:

Nicholas Arthur
Patrick Collins
Thomas Comyn (Lismore)
John Coppinger
Jasper Collins

Thomas Fitzgerald, Rostellan
Edmond Gough
James Gorman
Richard Gough
Nicholas Gallwan
Gerald Fitzgerald, Dromany
Richard Nagle
William Portingale
Thomas Prendergast
Theobald Ronane
James Ronane
Widow Uniacke
David Walsh

The sound of that nail being hammered through that piece of paper was like a nail in a coffin for those named. Under the act all men, women and children were to transplant to Connaught before 1 May 1654. Those who refused faced execution or banishment to the West Indies as slaves. But the government found enormous practical difficulties in implementing this policy: the numbers wanting to settle in Ireland were much smaller than had been hoped. Many of the soldiers, in time, sold their allotments of land to adventurers.

The Irish – peasants and gentry – were stubborn to move. Winter was setting in and the crops they had managed to plant that spring would be lost. How would they feed themselves, arriving in Connaught in mid winter? Large numbers refused to move, as if they did they would certainly perish. The government eventually revised its plan: only the landowners would move, estimated at about 2,000 families in total. In any case, the authorities needed to keep the ploughmen, herdsmen and labourers if the new Protestant landlords were to revitalise the farms.

The authorities had another problem in accurately determining the amount of land available on the island. If the requirements of the adventurers, soldiers and those to be transplanted were to be met, this question had to be answered. A survey of all lands to be forfeited was undertaken. Dr Benjamin Worsley was put in charge. Commissioners were dispatched round the country to take account of all the land at the disposal of the government. It was a humiliating and heartrending experience for the Uniackes to see commissioners survey the lands of Ballyvergin – the sole purpose being confiscation. It came to be known as the Civil Survey, but it had many flaws, and was followed by the Down Survey.

Dr William Petty, physician to the army in Ireland, undertook the second survey. As surveyor general, Petty produced an extremely accurate survey. The fieldwork was done by foot soldiers who, now that the war was over, had much time on their hands. By this stage, some 10,000 soldiers had been disbanded and were roaming the countryside.

The Uniackes appealed against the order to transplant. The government stipulated that only those who could prove they had shown 'constant good affection' towards parliament during the rebellion and Cromwellian war would be spared. For a Catholic, royalist family such as the Uniackes this task would be impossible.

The country was divided into 12 precincts, each managed by a commissioner. Heads of families liable to transplant were to give details to the commissioners in their area – names of families, particulars of tenants prepared to transplant with them, their age, colour of hair, height, distinguishing characteristics. Those to forfeit lands in Youghal were to report to the commissioner in Cork city. The Uniackes, like many of the others listed to transplant, simply stayed – at least until their appeals were heard by the judiciary. English Catholics would not be welcome by the Gaelic Irish in Connaught.

The flow of petitions slowed the resettlement, and the final date for departure came and went. Those who obeyed the order to transplant were sending back alarming reports. There was not enough land to meet the numbers to be transplanted (transplantees were entitled to two-thirds the lands of their original holdings) and much of that land was very poor quality.

By November 1654, the government was becoming concerned and issued the order: everyone liable to transplant must be gone by 1 March the following spring. Those who refused to transplant faced the death penalty. And on 19 March court marshals were set up to prosecute those still refusing to transplant. The Uniackes used the common defence: that their appeal had still to be heard.

Not all the establishment was in favour of the transplantation policy. The Protestant Co. Cork landlord, Vincent Gookin, who later became the member of parliament for Youghal, wrote a pamphlet attacking the government's programme. He published it anonymously in 1655. In it, he stated that banishing the Irish to Connaught would prove counterproductive, as it would place them among their fellow Gaels and give them greater advantage to rebel again:

> ... furthest remove from England, and for the sea shore most remote from the course of the English Fleet, where therefore they may receive arms from any foreign prince with most security ... The unsettling of a nation is an easy job, the settling is not, it has cost much blood and treasure there, and now prudence and mercy may accomplish the work ...

In October 1655, the Uniackes received a copy of a document from the authorities in Dublin, replying to the family's appeal against forfeiture:

> By the Lord Deputy and Council – upon reading a petition presented unto this board by Margaret Uniacke, widow, setting forth her deceased husband, Maurice Uniacke, his constant and faithful adherence to the English Interest, and his endeavours for the suppression of the rebels, and, therefore praying that a small estate near Youghal, belonging to her and her ancestors before her, may be granted unto her for the relief of herself and children, and the lease made thereof by the State might be revoked, and upon consideration had

thereof, and of a report from several officers of the army (signed by Sir Hardress Waller in the name of the rest) unto whom it was referred to certify their opinions what they conceived to be done therein, whereby the civil and faithful deportment of ye petitioner's husband towards ye English appears, ye same being said also attested a large certificate from several English and Protestants in about Youghal, and therefore certifying it as their opinion, that ye least favour which can in equity and conscience be showed her is that she should be continued in ye possession of her land, until ye qualification of those persons of ye town of Youghal were tried, and that then her condition, which to them seemed different from others, might have a special consideration, we do agree unto ye said report, and accordingly order that ye said Margaret Uniacke do continue the possession of ye said land in and near Youghal for ye subsistence of herself and family, paying Contribution until ye qualification of the inhabitants of ye said town shall receive a trial, at which time her condition shall be especially considered of by this board, and such further order given therein as shall be conceived fit.

Dated at Dublin Castle, 5 September 1655.
SIGNED: Thomas Herbert
Clerk of the Council

It was the following August before the family's petition was heard. The court of appeal sat at Mallow in north Co. Cork. At last, the Uniackes would receive some justice – or at least know their fate. Since the war ended in 1652 they had run the estate as best they could in order to survive and provide for when they might have no land to support them. During this period, life assumed a certain degree of mundane triviality. An entry in *The Council Book of Youghal* gives a rare glimpse of this: in September 1653 the local magistrates made a presentment against the widow, Margaret Uniacke, for failing to keep the area in front of her home clean, 'by reason the street is full of dung.'

On the morning of 5 August 1656, the market house in Mallow buzzed with activity. Many other families from Youghal were to receive their verdict at the Mallow sitting. A hushed silence descended upon the room as the three judges, in their black garb, entered. The chief judge was John Cook, one of the lawyers who had signed Charles II's death warrant: a scribble of ink that cost him his own life after the Restoration. Cook was a puritan with a burning desire to reform the legal system. He believed passionately in justice for the little man. And he had little time for papists or royalists, so the prospects for the appeals were not good. Case after case was reviewed. In the seventeenth century, there was no legal representation so the individual applicants had to argue their own cases. Margaret Uniacke and her son, Thomas, took turns to plead for leniency. Most of the cases were identical: how the claimant's family had remained loyal to parliament in the face of the Irish rebellion. And they had Protestant witnesses to prove it.

In all instances, the loyalty of these citizens was accepted. But 'they continued to reside in these towns [Youghal, Mallow, Kinsale and Cork] during the Inchiquin relapse from the Commonwealth to the king in 1648'. The commissioners reported that they had not demonstrated 'constant good affection ... but the law will be clear for them to have two parts in Connaught.' There was uproar. The prospect of being sent to Connaught resulted in near riot. One man shouted from the crowd that he would prefer to be shipped to Barbados as a slave than take up land in the western part of Ireland. They would be at the mercy of the Gaelic Irish, who detested them for being English. The remarks underlined the dilemma for Catholics of English stock: they were hated by the Irish for being English, and by the English for being Catholic. The incident led to a compromise: the Old English inhabiting the southern coast towns would not have to transplant. Instead, they would be granted lands in the baronies of Muskerry and Barrymore. The spectre of Connaught had faded.

For the time being, the Uniackes remained in their ancestral home. They had been spared the abyss of Connaught. The baronies of Barrymore or Muskerry would at least be less hostile and the soil more fertile – even if it were two-thirds of the old estate. The family was now preparing itself for the inevitable. It seemed that matters were settled. Maybe the Uniackes could get on with the job of farming, as their family had done for hundreds of years. Their material status might be reduced from wealthy landlord to tenant, but at least they would not be destitute.

It was not until 1657 that the Uniackes were ordered to remove themselves from their native town and transplant to Muskerry. Only then did the reality set in. Their lands and houses were let out to Thomas Vaughan and Joseph Murdock for 31 years at a rent of £190 3s 0d. They sublet parts of the property and land to other individuals in the town. There were newcomers to the town as well as long established Protestant families, who took possession of houses and gardens: Nicholas Stoute, Dr Blackwall, Alexander Greene, Simon Laughly, Thomas Warren, alderman Meeres, alderman Cox, William Baker, Thomas Baker, Abraham Vaughan and Edward Woods. It appears from the surviving documents that the Uniacke family was allowed to retain a small amount of land in the town. In return, they would manage the estate, bring it back to profit and provide an income for the new owners. They received six houses in Youghal, two of them with gardens and one with a 'backside', also two additional gardens and one pair of walls. Furthermore, the Uniackes retained two parcels of land in a place called Gortlangady, and two houses in the town of Kinsale. The Uniackes accepted their new role; they had little choice. Muskerry was alien, the quality of any land unknown. In any case, they had no capital to buy new stock. If they stayed put they might have some chance of getting their lands back if circumstances changed.

Religious oppression gathered momentum. A further statute was introduced – the Oath of Abjuration. All suspected Catholics had to take it: those who refused faced further confiscation of land. It is unlikely that Thomas or his mother took the oath, neither were they forced to do so by the authorities in Youghal.

But many of their fellow Catholics complied. It must have been a spectacle of puritan pageantry, large crowds gathering around the market cross within view of the Uniacke home. The puritan preacher in Youghal during the commonwealth, James Woods, would stand before them and call out the names of those to take the oath. Individuals would read from a parchment held before them. If they could not read, they repeated the words after the preacher. The oath stated:

> I _____ abhor and abjure the authority of the Pope as well in regard of the Church in general, as in regard of myself in particular. I condemn and anathematise the tenet that any reward is due to good works. I firmly believe and avow that no reverence is due to the Virgin Mary, or to any other saint in Heaven, and that no petition of adoration can be addressed to them without idolatry. I assert that no worship reverence is due to the sacrament of the Lord's Supper or to the elements of bread and wine after consecration, by whomsoever that consecration may be made. I believe there is no purgatory but that it is a popish invention, so is also the tenet that only the Pope can grant indulgences. I also firmly believe that neither the Pope nor any other priest can remit sins, as the papists rave. And all this I swear.

Thomas Uniacke of Ballyvergin inherited this world. He was of the old gentry but heir to nothing – a tenant from a family of lords.

5

Restoration of Hope

On 3 September 1658, Oliver Cromwell, the man blamed for the plight of the Irish, died. Within two years, the House of Stuart was restored to the throne of England. Without Cromwell's strength, there was no unified republican opposition.

The 28-year-old King Charles II had sympathies for the Catholic religion: his mother Henrietta Maria was a Catholic. So would the Uniackes and other 'Old English' Catholics be returned to their former status? It seemed unlikely. Charles I had always reneged on his promises in the face of opposition from Protestants, both in Britain and in Ireland. Charles II exhibited a similar trait. In order to enlist the support of Scottish Presbyterians against Cromwell he betrayed his Irish allies.

Oliver Cromwell was replaced by his son, Richard, who ruled England briefly. Soon English political society descended into chaos and in August 1659 the royalist general, Sir George Booth, led an uprising against the puritan republic. But the rebellion did not go as planned: Booth was defeated, and Charles' landing on English soil was cancelled. In October, General John Lambert overthrew parliament, though no one knew what would replace it. The race to fill the power vacuum left by Cromwell's death was on: General George Monck in Scotland disapproved of Lambert's actions and marched on London with his regiment. While Monck was a parliamentarian, and fought against the royalists in the civil war, Charles II believed he could be persuaded to back the return of the monarchy. Tentative approaches were made, but Monck was playing his cards close to his chest. On 3 February 1660, Monck's army entered London and restored order. Monck eventually declared his support for Charles, who until that time was not sure if the Scottish general really wanted to become, as Cromwell, the lord protector of his kingdom. Charles II entered London on 29 May. Huge crowds lined the streets to see him, the roads strewn with flowers, buildings hung with tapestries, church bells chiming.

The 1650s was a changed world for Thomas Uniacke, dramatically different to the one his father knew. In the Protestant-dominated towns, Catholicism was always treated with suspicion by the Protestant authorities, if not with downright persecution. Though there were exceptions and in Youghal Catholics had land and wealth, their political power was shrinking. Maurice Uniacke had held public office during the 1630s and had been a respected member of society. The Church still functioned: Masses were said, and the other sacraments administered, the young were educated and the catechism taught. Catholic marriages, baptisms and burials were openly practised, though a fee had to be paid to the Established Church.

Thomas had grown up in a world where the Catholic Church was not in a privileged position. But its situation could have been far worse. There were structural problems and difficulties implementing the religious renewal and reforms initiated by the Catholic Counter Reformation Council of Trent. The quality of the priests left a lot to be desired. A contemporary member of the hierarchy, Bishop Comerford of Waterford, said they were undisciplined and seldom catechised. 'They say Mass in the morning, then wander from house to house ... playing, drinking and vagabonding.' Synods of bishops spoke of backward people and ignorant clergy.

The bishops had set down the requirements for clergy at the synod of 1614. They decreed there had to be catechism every Sunday and a sermon where possible. Special attention had to be given to catechesis for children to prepare them for first confession at seven or eight, and first communion at twelve. The priest had to be able to teach the basics: Apostles' Creed, Lord's

Prayer and Ave Maria. Traditional patron days or 'patterns' were occasions for feasting and drinking, according to the hierarchy. Quite often, no Mass or prayers were said at these ceremonies. The excessive drinking and disorder associated with pilgrimages and wakes was attacked, as was the tradition of keening, a wailing performed at funerals. One episcopal conference described wakes in particularly colourful language, being full of 'jesters, bawdy songs, wanton mimes and other dark filthy works of darkness'. There were quarrels between diocesan and regular clergy that only helped to lower the estimation of clergy in the eyes of the laity. For example, friars feared bishops would gain control over their pastoral activities far beyond the norms laid down by general Church law.

In areas where propertied Catholics were few, Masses were said in sheds, outhouses and even in the open. In other areas, they were celebrated in the homes of the Catholic gentry. In many places, such as Youghal, the Catholic community built their own 'Mass houses' or chapels. Some were quite elaborate, as one description confirms:

> The pulpit in the church was richly adorned with pictures, and so was the high altar, which was advanced with steps, and railed out like a cathedral; upon either side thereof was erected places for confession; no fastened seats were in the middle or body thereof, nor was there any chancel; but that it might be more capacious, there was a gallery on both sides and at the lower end.

Mass was a time of private prayer for the congregation, with the priest at the altar performing the ritual, in an act that was essentially his own not theirs. 'Rites of Passage' – baptism, marriage and death – were more deeply rooted in the lives of the laity. Catholics placed great importance on being buried in monastic cemeteries. The remains of the holy dead consecrated a cemetery. Such holy neighbours would put one in good stead on the Last Day. But this was another fault line between secular and regular clergy. A fee had to be paid to the parish priest, even though the funeral was on old monastic soil – and now belonged to the Established Church.

With the arrival of Cromwell, everything had changed. The 1650s saw the destruction of the Catholic Church. The parish system, founded after the Council of Trent, collapsed completely. Prelacy and popery were banned as contrary to scripture. The object was the total elimination of the Catholic clergy. It is estimated that 1,000 priests fled to Europe. Others were transported to the West Indies or executed. Though the early enthusiasm for killing priests did soften, those priests who remained in Ireland hid in woods and caves, or travelled in disguise. Whatever progress had been made in teaching the Roman Catholic religion was nullified by the political events of the 1650s.

Christianity had always lived alongside the Celtic pagan religion and its customs which were alien to those of English extraction like the Uniackes. The ordinary people had lost contact with their priest. The native Irish were always quick to assume aspects of the earlier beliefs, or to blend them with Christianity. Pagan superstition was common among the peasantry, whose understanding of Catholic instruction was seriously lacking. Though most of them fervently supported the Roman Catholic Church, they were often ignorant of its teachings. There was serious confusion about the Holy Trinity, some of the peasants professing to believe in four persons in the one God: the Father, the Son, the Holy Ghost, and the Blessed Virgin.

Occasionally a travelling priest might pass through an area, and Mass would be held secretively and after dark. The word was passed round there was to be Mass and confession at a certain place at a certain time. After sunset, especially in the summer months when the work in the fields was finished the devout would set out. They never travelled in crowds. Moonless or cloudy nights were ideal as they gave the participants cover. The faithful would gather in a clearing, and then the priest – dressed in his vestments – would emerge from the bracken. A large rock or an improvised table was used as the altar, where the priest would place his gold chalice, cross and candlesticks. As he recited the Latin Mass, the congregation would mutter their own prayers. Afterwards he would hear confessions. Then his flock would disappear in the ancient oak forest. The priest would don his disguise and be gone. But many of these travelling 'priests' were uneducated, and had only a rudimentary grasp of Church doctrine.

The devout Thomas Uniacke was isolated and embittered by the experiences of puritan rule. The destruction of his religion was probably more painful than the forfeiture of his estates. He would have missed the guiding force of the Church and the education provided by orders such as the Franciscans. This ecclesiastical structure, which had still survived to some extent up to 1649, was now demolished – the clergy were dead or had fled. The secular parish priest in Youghal, Fr Jasper Gallwan, a family friend, had been an immeasurable source of guidance and strength. Maurice Uniacke had left the priest thirty shillings to pray for his soul in purgatory.

Priests were among those deported to the Caribbean as slaves. Thomas heard of harrowing scenes at ports such as Waterford where prisoners were put onto ships destined for the West Indies, their families watching helplessly from the quay. But most pitiful of all were the orphaned or abandoned children, whimpering inconsolably, being led up the gangplanks, looking behind in the desperate hope of seeing a lost parent who might come to their rescue at the very last minute. With manacled arms and legs, wearing filthy rags and covered in lice, the prisoners were packed below deck for the long journey to Barbados. The journey took several weeks and many died of typhus on the way. The crew would haul the corpses through the hatches and fling them ignominiously into the Atlantic. At night, the prisoners could hear the crew singing and drinking, as the slaves sat in their own excrement and vomit, which had caked hard on their skin and clothes by the time they reached the Caribbean. Eventually the ship dropped anchor in Spike's Bay. This was the first time the 'cargo' was allowed on deck. Before them was the green canopy of trees, silky white beaches, and whitewashed buildings. Instead of timber beams above their heads, they could see the clear blue sky, which at dusk became a blazing orange. The next day the planters came aboard and selected the slaves for the tobacco and cotton plantations. Life was hard for the labourers. They had to work from before dawn until the sun went down. From the morning onwards they were given no food or water, only a paltry meal after dark. They had to work under the parching sun, without shirts or shoes. Many of the Irish ran away from the plantations and lived by their wits in the wild. When captured they were whipped and returned to their owners. The Irish were mistrusted by the English authorities, and derided by the negroes, who called them the 'white slaves'.

By 1660, James Uniacke's religious and political allegiances had moved towards Protestantism and away from the traditional beliefs of his ancestors. Indeed, to James, religion was in essence political. The move was certain to create a great chasm in his family. Yet, there was no alternative. James had nothing and would have to make his own way in the world – and that could only be done as a Protestant. He decided he would study law, a profession that offered considerable opportunity. First, he would have to abandon the faith of his ancestors, and swear the Oath of Abjuration. This did not present a moral problem for James – for his conscience was decided. The first thing he had to do was find favour with the Protestant establishment.

Thomas Uniacke was incensed with his brother's decision. Cromwell had marched into their town, their country, profaned religious shrines and places of worship, outlawed the Roman Catholic Church, murdered or exiled her priests and introduced a draconian policy of transplantation and deportation. The puritans had reduced the Uniacke family, a once-noble family stretching back centuries, to paupers. And they had executed the sovereign king. To his family James was a lost soul. But to the Protestant establishment he would have been seen as a young convert repulsed by the superstition and idolatry of popery and set on his own spiritual salvation. They would have seen a clean-living, upright, hardworking young man.

One thing Thomas and his brother would have agreed on was the hope born of the Restoration – Thomas for justice, James for opportunity. An infectious air of festivity spread through Youghal with the news of Charles' return. The taverns were full and crowds spilled over into the streets. Streamers and tapestries hung from the windows of the houses on the main street. The recently replaced bells of St Mary's rang out with gusto.

Thomas joined in the celebrations. And as usual, he placed all his hopes, naively, in the mercy of the Stuarts.

BOOK TWO

A Family Divided

In January 1661, James Uniacke became a student in Trinity College Dublin. The only evidence for his time at the university is this entry in the Matriculation Book:

> *Dies Mensis – Januarii 28th, 1661. Pupillus – Jacobus Unicke. Parens – Mauritii Filius, Armigeri. Aetus – 20 Annor. Ubi Natus, Yeoghall, Coreagii. Ubi Educatus – Yeoghall. Tutor – Joseph Wilkins.*

That winter would most likely have been his first time to go any distance from Youghal. He was embarking on a lonely and dangerous adventure, but one that would ultimately win him status and wealth. When he set off for Dublin his financial means were unknown. His father had left him 'one stone house or messuage in Youghal ... and five enclosures or meadows of land'. It is not known if he had access to these assets in the 1660s. If he had converted before the confiscation of lands, he may have retained them, and they would have provided the means towards his college education.

Ireland was a lawless country in this period. Travelling was a perilous undertaking for anybody. Dispossessed Catholics called tories stalked the highways. Twenty-year-old James Uniacke had to make this life-changing and life-endangering journey. He probably crossed the river Blackwater on the ferry from Youghal, then travelled north over the easy terrain to Cappoquin. The route would have been largely empty of people, being winter, since there was little to do in the fields. Signs of the war, famine and plague that had devoured the country ten years earlier could be seen everywhere – abandoned fields, cottages with their roofs and doors collapsed. A traveller could ride for hours without seeing a single soul. Nor is it likely he would come across an inn before nightfall. Accounts of the time tell of how a peasant's cabin might be the only place to rest until morning. A cabin was usually a windowless thatched-roof building, entered through a low door. The visitor found himself in a smoke-filled room with no chimney, in the middle of a large poor Gaelic family who could not speak a word of English. The guest would be welcomed with pipe and whiskey and invited to join in a meal of potatoes served on a wooden platter accompanied by a bowl of sour milk. The guest was given the one bed in the house, often the only piece of furniture. A blanket was hung from the roof, dividing the room, allowing the visitor some privacy. The host family slept on the straw-covered earthen floor in front of the turf fire. Breakfast was more potatoes and milk. Sometimes the family would provide eggs, butter and potato cakes to sustain the traveller for the coming day.

The journey to Dublin would have taken several days. The most likely route was through Clonmel, Kilkenny, Leighlin Bridge, Carlow, Timolin, Old Kilcullen and Naas. In the bigger towns, accommodation was more substantial. The traveller had a proper room and could dry his clothes. In the bar, he could sit and eat a meal of mutton washed down with a bottle of claret, and listen to the conversation. Often other travellers would be talking about reports of tories on the road to Dublin and the safest route to avoid them.

There must have been periods of lonely terror for the young James Uniacke: the noise of a crow in the trees would make him jump; the sound of a twig breaking could be the foot of his attacker. The route skirted Coillaughtim Forest, one of the last remaining areas of extensive woodlands in the country; since Elizabethan times the English had been cutting down the ancient Irish oak to build their navy and supply charcoal for their iron industry. The only sound of human life would be the distant noise of chopping or the occasional cart carrying logs, passing him on the road and on any day, he would see only the occasional rider or carriage. Towards the latter stages of his journey, the Wicklow Mountains came into view on his right, dark and bleak in the depths of winter and he would have known his journey was near its end. This trip brought him through hundreds of years of Irish history: the medieval city of Kilkenny, with its twelfth-century Norman castle, still showing the scars of the Cromwellian attack; other walled market towns such as Clonmel and Carlow, still very much of the Middle Ages; across wastelands of scrubland and abandoned fields; past old pre-Christian Celtic hill forts, crumbling ivy-clad castles and tomb-like deserted churches and monasteries.

The new arrival to the metropolis would have encountered the wizened heads of some anonymous criminals or rebels hanging on poles above the city gate, and the cries of prisoners in the city's gaol, as they stretched their arms out of the barred windows begging passers-by to give them food or money. The buildings on the narrow streets of Dublin were similar to those in Youghal: gable fronted, with the top storey jutting out over the ground floor. Busy markets took place in the confined spaces, lit up by the thin strips of sky above them, while citizens argued and dogs tussled over a dead carcass. The lingering smells of Dublin, more pungent and sickening in the height of summer, became familiar to the newcomer – the stench of rotten meat or crusted sewage building up in the roughly cobbled streets. James quickly became acquainted with the small compact medieval city. It seemed that every second premises was a tavern where punters could eat as much as they wanted – beef and potatoes, or Dublin Bay oysters caught fresh that morning – for every two pennyworth of beer they bought. Rising above all this were the spires of Christ Church and St Patrick's cathedral, and of course the towers of Dublin Castle, seat of English rule in Ireland since the thirteenth century. The castle dominated the whole city, with its thick walls, sturdy towers and deep moat.

The city of Dublin was built on a ridge along the south bank of the river Liffey. By 1660, it was already expanding beyond its medieval walls. A single bridge traversed the wide tidal river to the suburb of Oxmantown; meadows and fertile pastures; clumps of ancient oak forest; St Michan's church and the ruins of St Mary's, the old Cistercian monastery, destroyed after the Reformation. James Uniacke probably knew very little about his capital's history. But the city would become his home at a time of great historic change.

We do not know where James Uniacke stayed while a student in Dublin. He may have stayed in the college itself. But he did have a relative in Dublin, a merchant called Henry Uniacke, whose name never came up in any of the family documents or histories, but is mentioned in city records.

James Uniacke's place of study was outside the city walls, an impressive redbrick building with railings at the front. There was a garden just inside the entrance arch with a panoramic view of the river Liffey and the sails of the vessels docked along its banks and quays. An elegant terrace faced on to the scene. A large oak tree in the middle of the garden acted as a sundial in sunny weather, casting its shadows across the flowerbeds. But James Uniacke was not there to admire the beauty or to socialise. He proved to be an exemplary pupil. Throughout his time at university, he watched political events unfold. Since the monarchy was restored in England hope had grown that King Charles II would return the lands that had been forfeited by Cromwell. While the king had sympathy towards the Catholic religion he was reluctant to upset Protestant opinion, both in Ireland and in England. Leading Protestants like Coote and Broghill, who had fought against the royalists in the civil war, wanted the Cromwellian settlement retained. The arrival back in Ireland of Ormonde as Charles' new viceroy in the country, spelled the best hope for a compromise that might satisfy the opposing demands of land ownership.

James Uniacke's instinct was that the Old English Catholic gentry would never regain its former position. Since the days of the Reformation, Protestantism had been tightening its grip on power. That process would continue. The Irish parliament called by the king in 1661 was entirely Protestant. However, it did pass the Act of Settlement, enacting in law Charles' desire to see justice for 'innocent Catholics'. The act allowed for the setting up of a court of claims, which would sit in Dublin. James was encouraged. For a man who wanted to be a lawyer he saw that his family could make a legal challenge to the confiscation of their lands. There may have been an element of guilt as well as family loyalty in his motives.

While his fellow students revelled in the taverns, he studied the legislation. Catholics who could prove their innocence before the commissioners would have their properties restored to them immediately – without the Protestant proprietors being compensated. The names of the claimants were to be published, and time allowed Cromwellian planters to appoint an attorney to act in their defence. If both plaintiff and defendant agreed that the plaintiff owned land before 1641, all that had to be established was their innocence in the rebellion of the 1640s. James was cautious, but felt his family would have a good case. Yet he realised the current holders of the estate would most likely challenge both claim to innocence and land title. All claims would have to be submitted by 5 November 1662.

James Uniacke witnessed the flowering of Restoration Dublin with the arrival of the duke of Ormonde on 27 July 1662 as the new viceroy of Ireland. The age saw the transformation of Dublin into a modern European city. Its new architecture symbolised a new age and burgeoning self-confidence. The Irish Renaissance was the world where James Uniacke studied and practised as a lawyer, and made himself a leading member of Dublin society.

The significance of Ormonde's return could not have been

lost on the astute and gifted young man. The popularity of the duke was evident from the popular response to his arrival back in Dublin. On that summer morning crowds made their way out of the city – the poor on foot, the rich on horseback or in carriages. They were headed for Howth, the peninsula that formed the northern arm of Dublin Bay. They gathered on the slope of Howth that looked down on the small fishing village of the same name. A large crowd had assembled, sitting on the rocks and the heather. Not far beyond the harbour entrance was a tiny island – more like a boulder – called Ireland's Eye. Towards the horizon was a larger more fertile island, called Lambay Island. A large man-of-war was anchored near the harbour entrance, its sails stowed. A pinnace was moored alongside. The crowd saw the figure of Ormonde emerge on the deck of the ship to rapturous applause.

During the period James was studying in Trinity, his hometown had been gripped by the notorious witch trial of Florence Newton, which had struck fear into its inhabitants. He heard about the case, the accounts having spread the length and breadth of the country. There can be no doubt that his relatives in Youghal were caught up in the hysteria, and probably held opinions of what fate the woman should suffer. The trial was so significant that the attorney general, Sir William Domville, led the prosecution.

Rumours had been rife in Youghal that a coven of witches was active in the town and a team of witch finders – Messrs Perry and Greatrakes and Dr Blackwell – were trying to track them down.

In March 1661, the activities of Florence Newton attracted their attention. Stories had been circulating of a dispute between herself and a servant called Mary Longdon. In a deposition, Longdon said Newton came to her master's house at Christmas 1660, and asked for some beef out of the powdering tub. The request was refused and Newton became angry and went away grumbling: 'Thou had'st as good give it me.' A week later, the two met at the well in North Main Street. Newton ran at Longdon and threw aside the pail she was carrying on her head. Then she kissed Longdon violently saying, 'I pray let thou and I be friends; for I bear thee no ill will, and I pray thee do thou bear me none.' To which Longdon fled away in terror.

A few nights later, the servant woke to see a veiled woman standing at the end of her bed and, beside her, a small man dressed in silk clothes, which Longdon took to be a spirit. He drew back the veil to reveal the face of Newton. Then, with a grin, he turned to Longdon and said she could have anything she wanted if she trusted in him. To which Longdon replied: 'I trust in the Lord.'

Within a month, Longdon fell ill, having fits and trances. It took three or four men to hold her down. Word passed round the town that she was bewitched and having fits in which she vomited up needles, pins, horse nails, wool and straw. As she lay in bed stones would fall upon her. Even as she walked about the house, she would be pelted on the head, shoulders and arms. Several witnesses claimed to have seen this. The objects would appear from the ceiling, hit the victim, then disappear again. In her despair, Longdon would call out Newton's name, imploring her to stop the torment. Stories that Newton had bewitched the woman soon spread.

John Payne, Longdon's master, contacted the witch finders. The three men came one wet, windy night in March. By candle-light, they ascended the narrow creaky stairs to the top of the house. The howling of the victim resonated through the building. They entered the small attic room where Longdon lived. There on the bed the middle-aged woman writhed and scream-ed, her eyes bulging out of their sockets. Her mind rambled and her eyes became fixed on the corner of the room. She saw an apparition of Florence Newton who approached and jabbed her violently with a long pin. Longdon gasped and yelled in agony, calling out Newton's name, begging her to cease the torment. The men could see nothing, but did feel an evil presence.

Next day Newton was arrested on the order of the mayor, and taken to the town prison. There the mayor questioned her. She denied bewitching Longdon, pointed the finger at two other women, Goodwife Halfpenny and Goodwife Dod, and said that they had the real powers to bewitch. That night a group of men, including Edward Perry, the witch finder, visited Newton in her cell. Under interrogation, she continued to deny the charge. She fell on her knees and begged God's forgiveness if she had done anything to harm Longdon. At that instant, the door of the prison shook and Newton stood up and said, as if to someone in the room: 'What makest thou here this time of night'. The room filled with a loud noise, as if chains were being hit against the walls. Then silence descended. In considerable haste, Perry and some others then took a tile from the prison roof and brought it to the cell, placed it on Newton's forehead, and quickly left.

They brought the tile to Payne's house and put it in the fire until it was red hot. Lifting it out with thongs Perry poured some water on it. At that moment, the guards in the gaol were reported to have heard Newton cry out in pain. Determined to get a confession, the men returned to the gaol to fetch the witch. They dragged her through the dark streets. A fierce gale was blowing, as if some malevolent force was trying to stop them getting to their destination. Finally, they reached the home of Nicholas Stoute in Friar Street. Stoute was a shoemaker, and was renowned for his knowledge of witchcraft and how to combat it. Stoute brought them into his workshop at the back where Newton was roughly put on to a stool. Throughout she never said a word. The interrogation continued, and the shoemaker suggested the awl. One of the inquisitors, the witch finder Blackwell, plunged the sharp metal instrument at her hand, but it did not penetrate. A second attempt succeeded, and blood poured down the old woman's lap, drenching her petticoat and dripping on the floor between her feet. She was returned to the gaol, her screams waking the town.

Next day Newton was brought to the tholsel for further questioning by the mayor. Newton was pulled through the crowd that lined Main Street, a dirty bloodstained rag wrapped round her hand. Her head was bowed. But no one was brave enough to stare for long – in case her eyes would look up and meet theirs. Halfpenny and Dod were also brought there. The mayor decided that since Newton had not confessed to the charge, the 'water experiment' should be done on all three of them. Under the test, the suspected witch would have her right thumb tied to her left great toe, and vice versa. Then she would be thrown into the water. If she sank, she was innocent, if she floated, she was guilty. The three women were taken to the gaol. Halfpenny and Dod protested their innocence. And Longdon, who was well enough to attend the experiment, spoke in their defence, saying Newton was the culprit. Three guards lifted the accused witch, a rope tied about her waist, into the water. As soon as she hit the surface, Perry cried out that she floated, and the men holding the rope pulled her back.

Newton was put in gaol, bolted and in chains. But tales of her powers continued to circulate, even spreading to other parts of the country. It was claimed she killed a David Jones. He and another man, Frank Besely, were standing sentinel outside the prison one night. They wanted to see if cats or other creatures entered through the grate into the prison cell. Jones felt himself lured to the bars, and called in to the old woman, challenging her to recite the Lord's Prayer. He got no response. A while later a voice called: 'David, come hither, I can recite the Lord's Prayer now.' It was Newton. Jones approached gingerly, Beseley stayed a safe distance behind. Foolishly, Jones placed his hand on the metal grate. Newton quickly kissed it with her withered lips and toothless gums.

The next day he confessed to his wife: 'She hath kissed my hand and I have a great pain in that arm. I verily believe she has bewitched me.' Later he fell ill and died within two weeks, crying out: 'The hag has me by the hand and is pulling off my arm. Do you not see the old hag, how she pulls me?'

At the Cork Assizes on 11 September 1661, Florence Newton met her accusers. The courtroom was packed, including many Youghal town folk, there as if to extirpate some deep fear that collectively gripped them. Autumn sunlight poured through the windows. There was an air of expectation, then a whisper ran through the crowd: the witch was being brought in. Surrounded by soldiers, the tiny woman was led in, the manacles on her feet and hands clanking in the silent room. Everyone stared at her, dicing with danger, ready to avert their eyes should she look their way. If that happened, the person would be bewitched. Then the frail figure of Mary Longdon took the stand and gave her evidence.

Halfway through her evidence the trial took a dramatic turn. Longdon glanced nervously at the defendant, who raised her manacled hands towards the plaintiff and shook them violently. Longdon collapsed and was carried out of the court. As she was being removed, she went into a fit and it took several strong men to contain her. 'Now she is done', Newton was heard to mutter. The judge ordered that the bolts be put back on the accused, to which she cried out that she was being killed.

When the case resumed the other witnesses gave their accounts. After Nicholas Stoute gave his evidence, he suggested that Newton be commanded to say the Lord's Prayer, so the judge could see with his own eyes that the woman was a witch. Four times she attempted: 'Give us this day our daily bread ... and we forgive them ... ' Repeatedly she left out 'And forgive us our trespasses.' A preacher was appointed to teach her the words. But still she could not remember. This convinced the judge of her guilt, and he sentenced her. The old woman became hysterical with what energy she still possessed. She protested that she was old and in bad memory. But that plea would not save her.

The eventual fate of poor Florence Newton is not recorded.

7

A Plea for Justice

The Court of Claims opened in January 1663 at the King's Inns in Dublin. Between then and the autumn almost one thousand cases were heard. James Uniacke spent much of his time at the sessions, which were always packed solid. He wanted to assess each of the seven commissioners, learn something about them: their attitudes, prejudices and personalities. The up-and-coming lawyer still had contact with his family, and he was willing to help them. It is likely he prepared the family petition for the court. A lot of his spare hours would have been spent at the Discrimination Office in the King's Inns, where all the documents relating to the court were deposited. Here the concerned parties could search for letters, examinations, orders, petitions, muster rolls and other material relating to their cases.

The remit of the court was to establish whether a family that had its lands confiscated had taken part in the rebellion that began on 22 October 1641. The Uniackes were in a position to prove this. Their case would emphasise that they, and other inhabitants of Youghal, had shown constant good affection towards the royalists, billeting the king's forces in their homes. The calls by the earls of Thomond and Inchiquin to restore the 'innocent Catholics' would also be cited. James could only speculate what defence the recipients of the land would make. The court could not pass judgement on land title, as that would have to be established in a different court.

On Monday 27 July 1663 the Uniacke petition was presented to the Court of Claims, perhaps symbolically a year to the day since the duke of Ormonde had set foot triumphantly back in Ireland. That day was a new beginning for Ireland, its first anniversary felt like a new beginning for the Uniackes. The entire family would have come to Dublin for the hearing at King's Inns. The petition was laid out precisely and in detail:

Thomas Uniacke, gentleman, and Margaret Uniacke, widow, claim the two plowlands of East and West Ballyvergin, liberties of Kinsale, county Cork; the half plowland of Borneegeehy; two houses and one garden in Youghal; One house more and one garden in Youghal, all now in the claimants' possession; one house and one garden in the possession of Dr Blackwall; one house and two gardens in the possession of Mr Stoute; one other house in Youghal in the possession of the claimants; one house and garden in the possession of Thomas Vaughan; one house and backside in the possession of Alexander Greene; one house and backside in the possession of Simon Laughly; two houses in the claimants' possession; one other pair of walls and a garden in the claimants' possession; one house and one backside more in the claimants' possession; two houses and two gardens in the possession of the said Mr Stoute; one house and garden in the possession of Thomas Warren; a house and garden in the claimants' possession; a plot of ground in the possession of Alderman Meeres; one other garden in the claimants' possession; four closes and three gardens in the possession of Alderman Cox; four closes in the possession of William Baker; two closes in the possession of Joseph Morducke; a plot of ground in the possession of Thomas Baker; three plots of ground in the possession of John Stoute; one plot of ground in the possession of Nicholas Stoute; one mill in the possession of John Stoute; three plots of ground in the possession of Abraham Vaughan; two plots of ground in the possession of Edward Woods; two parcels of land called Gortlangady in the possession of the claimants, all which premises are situate, lying and being within the liberties of Kinsale in the county of Cork.

Setting forth that Maurice Uniacke, late of Youghal, alderman, father of the claimant Thomas, and husband unto the claimant Margaret, was in his lifetime and on 22 October 1641 seized in fee or fee tail of and in all and singular the premises, and about December 1648 died so seized, whereby the third part of all and singular the premises and other the estate of inheritance fell and was vested in the claimant for life as her thirds and dower, and the reversion of the other two parts descended and came unto the claimant Thomas as eldest son and heir of the said Maurice, which is the claimants' title.

In proving they were 'innocent Catholics', the family's case would have been strengthened by the support they received from the Protestant community in Youghal. When the family lands were to be forfeited, many parliamentarian army officers, including Sir Hardress Waller himself, came to the defence of the Uniackes. Many Protestant folk of the town held the family in the highest regard. They had shown great loyalty towards the crown during the years of rebellion, suffering alongside their fellow Protestant townsfolk. The husband and father of the claimants had held public office as alderman, mayor and bailiff.

Surprisingly, the occupying landlords made no appeal against the petition. Perhaps they were confident they would not be forcibly removed from the estate, or that the crown would in time have to compensate them with alternative lands. But that was a problem for another day.

After a short deliberation, the commissioners gave their verdict: the family's petition had been accepted.

Thomas Uniacke had now regained all his agricultural land and most of his property in the town of Youghal. But it seemed there was unfinished legal business. On 7 November 1664, he issued a chancery bill to have a case heard against Edmond Fitzgerald of Rostellane. The case appears to have been thrown out because Edmond Fitzgerald was dead. A new case would have to be taken against the beneficiaries of his will. The following February Thomas presented another chancery bill before the court in Dublin to the Right Honorable Sir Maurice Eustace, Knight, lord chancellor of Ireland.

> *Humbly complaining show unto your Lordship your Orator Thomas Uniacke, otherwise Thomas Uniacke of Ballyvergin, son and heir of the said Maurice Uniacke, deceased.*
>
> *That Sir John FitzEdmond Gerald, late of Ballymoloe for forty or fifty years, or thereabouts, unjustly withheld from your said Suppliant, Thomas Uniacke, and his said ancestors and cousin whose heir he is, the ensuing lands, tenements and hereditaments in the*

county of Cork, and the said Sir John finding death to approach, did in discharge of his conscience, make and publish his last will and testament, and thereby did devise unto your said suppliant Thomas Uniacke and his heirs the plowland of Mucerice, the half plowland of Clashy Donagh, the half plowland of East Borneegeehy, and the lands of east Ballyvergin, which he by his said last will acknowledged to be the estate and inheritance of your said suppliant Thomas Uniacke and his cousin and ancestors whose heir he is.

Now so it, may it please your Lordship, that Sir John FitzEdmond Gerald of Rostellane, in the said county of Cork, son and heir of the said Sir John FitzEdmond Gerald the younger, hath immediately after the decease of his dead father ... possessed himself of the lands of Vansymore, Classydonagh, Borneegeehy, Ardnasacke and Ballyvaricke, and the same doth detain from your suppliant Thomas Uniacke; that also James Lavallin doth keep and detain from your Orator the said plowland of Mucerice; and Dame Mable Tent als. Osborne, and her now husband Roger Osborne, the lands of Ballyclennessy, being the undoubted inheritance of your suppliant Thomas Uniacke.

Thomas Uniacke had learned that he was being unjustly deprived of ancestral land. There is no evidence, but it seems probable that legal detective work on the part of his brother unearthed his legal entitlement. He must have been aware of the situation in July 1663, as the family's submission referred to their title of two of the disputed pieces of land, Borneegeehy and East Ballyvergin. According to the will of one James FitzThomas of Rostellane, dated 17 August 1635, and proved 12 November the same year, he instructed the executor to do the following:

I have and bequeath that Sir John Fitzgerald, knight, according to his better advisors may give unto Maurice Uniacke all such writings and papers as I have in my custody, that may be available for the gentleman and not a detriment to his own inheritance.

It was clear from the executor's will dated 1 September 1640, and still not proved at the time of the Court of Claims, that he had not done so. And, furthermore – admitted his guilt.

> I pray God Almighty to forgive me for the long concealment of this
> wrongfully and keeping and detaining and harbouring of my grand-
> father's will ... which was against the law of God and the world,
> God forgive me my mortal sins; and also the concealment of my
> cousin James Fitzgerald of Rostallane who desired me to leave his
> own land to Mr Thomas Uniacke of Youghal ... I must confess that
> I found no good prosperity for me doing the same for which I pray
> God forgive me my sins.

Then the will listed the lands in question: *'one plowland of Mucerice, half plowland of Clasidonie, the lands of Borneegeehy, and the
lands of East Ballyvergin.'*

Investigation of the legal history found that one of the Uniacke ancestors, a John Uniacke, made over large tracts of land
to a Thomas FitzGerald of Rostellane. The details were in an in-
quisition taken after the death of John Uniacke. It stated *'...
that the said John Uniacke, together with Phylis Annias als. Forrest,
of Youghal, widow, by their deed bearing date 8 September* AD *1609
conveyed to Thomas FitzGerald of Rostellane, in the said county, his
heirs and assigns, their whole right, title, etc., in the town and lands
of Mockerish.'* The reason for doing so was unclear, but James
could now prove that John FitzEdmond Gerald had wished the
lands in question to be returned to the Uniacke family.

Thomas Uniacke won his action. For a while, at least the
legal system gave him some justice.

Calm Between Storms

James Uniacke got employment as a junior attorney after leaving Trinity College. His aptitude for law soon built him a reputation. This was a busy time for lawyers, when fortunes could be made. The Restoration meant a huge amount of legal work: new title deeds had to be drawn up, old ones confirmed, and those grantees at risk of losing property had to be defended. James would act for either side – one man's money was as good as another's. Increasingly he began to move in the social circles of the metropolis. It was at this time he met his future wife. Her name was Mary Neale, daughter of James Neale, a merchant in St Werburgh's Parish. He was a wealthy man, having inherited his father's tallow chandling business.

The new social milieu of James Uniacke was in stark contrast to that of Youghal, where the taverns and rough outdoor sports were the extent of its culture. He would have been a frequent visitor to Smock Alley theatre near Dublin Castle. The interior of the theatre was well lit with lamps and candles, and had gilded galleries overlooking the stage. The city's rich were well insulated from the seedier aspects of the capital. Afterwards the playgoers would travel home in carriages and sedan chairs, barely negotiating the narrow streets. Out of taverns came boisterous laughter and the clank of drinking tankards. Pimps, muggers and prostitutes skulked in dark alleyways, while beggars – many of them children – would push their hands through carriage windows pleading for alms.

On 31 May 1665, James Uniacke and Mary Neale married at the parish church of St Werburgh's. None of his family attended the Anglican ceremony, not that James expected they would. At this time, James Uniacke was also developing political connections with Youghal. One important contact was Edward Perry, who passed on information that might be useful to the young lawyer. This was the same Perry who only three years before had had a hand in the prosecution of Florence Newton for being a witch. In the spring of 1666, he wrote to Uniacke with some interesting news: that Nicholas Stoute (also involved in the Newton trial) was rumoured to be involved in fraudulent activities. Perry promised to dig deeper. There was an ongoing legal dispute between the Uniackes and Stoute over property in the town. This presented an opportunity to exact revenge.

Thirty years before, Nicholas Stoute's father had leased property from the Uniackes and from the time of the rebellion had refused to pay any rent on the property. He had paid the subsequent grantees though. But once the Uniackes were restored as titleholders, payments ceased once again. Once James had proof of Stoute's activities, he could pressurise him on the disputed houses in the centre of Youghal. He proposed to his mother and brother that he receive the houses in lieu of payment for legal services to them. He was a young professional keen to make his fortune. Both Margaret and Thomas agreed. Stoute had little choice but to agree. The lease was assigned to James Uniacke. If Stoute thought he had bought James Uniacke's silence, he was wrong. On 4 December 1666, *The Council Book of Youghal* recorded the action taken by Uniacke and Perry. 'That Mr James Uniack(e) and Mr Edward Perry do apply themselves unto Sir William Davies desiring him that he confer with the king's attorney touching the Staple Charter [licence to trade in commodities such as wool] now detained by Mr Nicholas Stoute, and that he be compelled to bring it in. That Mr Uniack(e) shall act for the Corporation in this matter.'

During this time, Thomas and his mother strove to rebuild their estate, restocking the land with cattle. In 1669 Thomas, the heir of the Uniackes of Ballyvergin, decided to increase his estate and leased the lands of Ballycolloname from his Protestant rival, the earl of Cork. The estate had originally been owned by the Fitzgeralds, and came into the possession of Cork during the seventeenth century. A condition of the contract stuck in Uniacke's throat. He had to provide 'one able horse and horseman well armed to attend the said earl, his heirs, or assigns at all musters and general meetings for the service of ye crown and defence of the country.' But Thomas needed those lands to develop a beef cattle herd, so had no choice but to agree.

While Thomas was expanding, liquidity remained a problem. At the same time he was hoping to get married. His brother in Dublin was in a position to lend money, so it was to him that Thomas went. In a deed of mortgage, dated 7 April 1670, it is stated that 'Thomas and Margaret in consideration of the sum of £100, paid to them by the said James Uniacke of ye city of Dublin, made over to him four meadows or closes of land, within the liberties of Youghal, as security for the repayment of the said loan.'

Not long after, Thomas married Ellinor Fitzgerald of Lisquinlan. She was the eldest daughter of Garrett Fitzgerald of Co. Cork and sister and co-heir of the Right Honourable Robert Fitzgerald. Ellinor Uniacke bore her husband four children. The eldest was Margaret. Then came Thomas, his heir. Their third child was also a boy, James. The last baby was Ellinor, died in infancy.

The 1670s was not a bad time for Catholic landowners who were once again in possession of their estates. While they were allowed engage in commerce, they were generally excluded from political life. During the second half of the 1660s, Thomas, with help from his aging mother, strove to rebuild their stock. The Cattle Acts, which banned the export of Irish livestock, made the task difficult; though the export market for butter and meat expanded round the same time. During the 1670s Youghal became a leading Irish port for the export of butter, mainly to France and Flanders. Thomas watched the business grow. Soon he too was drawn into the butter trade.

Thomas Uniacke learned about managing a farm from family and friends. During the Cromwellian years, he found himself a tenant where his family had once been landlords. Yet farming was his only means of income, and his sole source of status, so he made the most of it. He would have placed great trust in his tenants, especially the older more experienced ones. The tenant was an invaluable asset and source of knowledge. When Thomas Uniacke attended the spring and autumn fairs, he needed a good husbandry man along with him. When buying a young heifer he needed someone who could identify a genuine springer that would be capable of calving. It was still a risky business. Cattle might not calve, might become sick or go dry. There were other uncontrollable elements: stock being stolen or killed by wolves, or simply getting lost. These factors eroded the profitability of even the most efficiently managed estate. To inject more capital into the business Thomas had to borrow extensively. In February 1679, he borrowed £2,000, a staggering amount for the time. This enabled him to invest in the estate: build additional dairies, purchase butter-making equipment, bowls and butter churns. He also had his overheads, salt to preserve produce and wood to make the butter barrels.

In the 1670s, religious persecution of Catholics was generally relaxed, though worship was still low key. In November 1673 the corporation of Youghal, now entirely in Protestant hands, voted 'that the gates to the town be locked on the Lord's day during Divine Service and Sermon, in the forenoon and afternoon'. In this atmosphere, Thomas Uniacke yearned for an age when English monarchs and all English colonists were Catholic. That hadn't been since Henry VIII broke with Rome in the sixteenth century. Thomas despaired he would never live to see the day that his fellow countrymen would revert to their old faith. In 1675, a second brother, John, converted to the Established Church and became a Protestant. He was a trader in Youghal, and on his conversion was admitted as a freeman of the town.

Religious and political tensions heightened for a time in the late 1670s. In November 1679 Oliver Plunkett, the Roman Catholic archbishop of Armagh, was arrested on charges of treason. He was a priest with many enemies, and not solely among Protestants and the English. He was tried in London, the authorities fearing he might be acquitted if the case was to be heard in Ireland. Oliver Plunkett had been made primate of Ireland in 1669, replacing Archbishop Edmund O'Reilly. Plunkett was a firm supporter of the European Counter Reformation, and believed the Church in Ireland needed to be revitalised from the top down. This differed from the traditional Gaelic view, that the Church needed regeneration from the ground upwards. The 1670s saw Catholic Ireland split into bitter factions. Plunkett, who was Old English Catholic, supported the civil authorities and the monarchy.

Plunkett came into conflict with the Franciscan order, which had strong support among both Old English and Gaelic Catholics. Jansenism, a movement founded by Cornelius Jansen in the early seventeenth century, heavily influenced the Franciscans. He was a Catholic theologian at the University of Louvain in the Spanish Netherlands and later became archbishop of Ypres, before dying in 1638. He had a close association with the Franciscans from a very early stage. Jansen studied St Augustine in great depth, and concluded that God's will was conferred on chosen individuals, and that there was no such thing as free will. He rejected the official Church position that God's grace was conferred on all, and the individual had the right to accept or reject it. He did not believe in the supremacy of the papacy and the universality of the Roman Catholic Church. His ideas were very close to Calvin's Predestination. The Church was determined to crush this heresy, and its biggest battalion against Jansenism were the Jesuits.

Jansenism had little relevance to Thomas Uniacke, though he politically and culturally identified with Plunkett. But Thomas' father had been a devotee of the Franciscans, and was buried in the habit of that order. Whether he had been a Jansenite, Thomas did not know. The rift between the Franciscan order and Archbishop Plunkett pained him. Yet, Thomas was nearer to Plunkett and the religious outlook of the Old English than he was to Jansenist-influenced Franciscans who represented continuity with Gaelic, Irish traditions. Plunkett was a supporter of royalty. The Jansenists, like their Calvinist opposites, justified regicide. This was something Thomas could never support. Indeed, Plunkett was probably the best representative of Thomas Uniacke's dream of a marriage between Catholicism and Monarchy. And he could only have been heartened and cheered by the primate's declaration of 1670:

> We, Your Majesty's subjects, the clergy of the Roman Catholic Church, do hereby declare and solemnly protest before God and his angels, that we own and acknowledge Your Majesty to be our lawful king and the undoubted monarch, as well of this realm of Ireland as of all other Your Majesty's dominions; and consequently we confess ourselves bound in conscience to be obedient to Your Majesty in all civil and temporal affairs ... and therefore we promise that we, during life, will inviolably bear true allegiance to Your Majesty, your lawful heirs and successors, and that no power on earth shall be able to withdraw us from our duty herein; and that we will, even to the loss of life and property, if occasion requires, assert and defend Your Majesty's rights against all that shall invade the same, or attempt to deprive Your Majesty, your lawful heirs and successors, of any part thereof ...

But the primate's fate was not to be set by events in Ireland. It was political events in England, aided by certain Franciscans, which led to Plunkett being arrested. The relative calm of Ireland was not reflected across the water. In 1673, the English parliament had overruled the Declaration of Indulgences, granted by Charles II to Catholics, which allowed them more religious freedoms. It also attempted to stop James II marrying a Catholic.

There was a paranoid atmosphere of conspiracy and intrigue. Then, in 1678, a man called Titus Oates revealed a conspiracy by Jesuits to organise a French invasion of England. A supporter of the Jesuits, Plunkett was easily linked to the conspiracy. King Charles was probably aware that Archbishop Plunkett was innocent, as no solid evidence was presented at the trial. But he did not act. In Ireland, Ormonde was coming under pressure from the English parliament to clamp down. He did not believe the Irish were about to rebel as part of a wider plot though. He felt the Irish would only rise up if there were panic among the Protestant population. But Ormonde did take certain precautions to allay fears. The army was put in a state of readiness. An order was issued for all Roman Catholic bishops and clergy to leave the kingdom. All Catholics were ordered to hand in their arms. There was increased fear and tension, but Ormonde made no moves to disarm Catholics. He refused to dispossess popish proprietors as potential rebel leaders, a stance that infuriated the English parliament.

Archbishop Oliver Plunkett was beheaded at Tyburn in July 1681, and became the last in a line of Catholic martyrs. When Thomas Uniacke read the pamphlet announcing the execution, he saw another example of how his fellow Englishmen would never tolerate any shade of Catholicism.

By the 1680s, James Uniacke had become one of the wealthiest lawyers in the metropolis. He and his family lived in a fashionable house in Back Lane overlooking the city walls and the crumbling towers, the spire of St Patrick's cathedral and beyond, the scenic Dublin Mountains. The couple had nine children: Margaret, James, Mary, Ann, Norman, Grace and Kearney, two other children, John and Stephen, died prematurely. John passed away in January 1670, just three months old. Stephen died on St Stephen's Day 1678, two days before his third birthday.

On 29 June 1682, James Uniacke dictated his last will and testament. He left to his eldest son, James, all his lands and property in the town and liberties of Youghal, as well as the lands of Inshinecrenagh, Carrigarostig, and Knockmacderry. James also inherited lands in Limerick and Waterford. James Uniacke enclosed a codicil that his wife would remain in the family home until her death and would be given a substantial annuity. As well as his legal business, James also had a thriving stationary trade. Within two weeks, James and Mary Uniacke would set off for England, to the spa town of Tunbridge Wells, south of London. It appears that James was in poor health, and this may have been a reason for organising his affairs before he left. Tunbridge, in Kent, was famous for its reddish-coloured, bubbling spring, which was said to have curative properties. It was a popular resort for courtiers, gentry and royalty suffering from various maladies. James Uniacke's wealth put him among them. But the waters could offer no cure for him. He never returned: on 10 August 1682, aged 41, he died and was buried the following day in the cemetery of St Peter and St Paul, Tunbridge parish church – a place of calm that could never be disturbed.

BOOK THREE

9

A Catholic King

In February 1685 King Charles II died, and was succeeded by his Catholic brother James II. Irish Catholics were jubilant. The Protestant population was alarmed. The appointment of Richard Talbot, earl of Tyrconnell, as lord deputy of Ireland gave substance to their fears. He was a staunch aristocratic Catholic, and determined to redress the plight of the Catholic faith. Tyrconnell set about restructuring the army in Ireland, replacing Protestant officers with Catholic. The civil administration was also transformed, not long after his arrival the majority of Protestant judges and privy counsellors were replaced by Catholics. Catholic sheriffs were provided for all counties. The corporation charters were called in by *quo warranto*, and new ones issued. These put the balance of power firmly in the hands of the Catholic population. Protestants became increasingly unsettled, many fled to England or Ulster where they outnumbered Catholics. However, King James was facing stiff opposition in England, where there was deep opposition to Catholicism. Support was growing for his Protestant rival, William of Orange, whose family came from the tiny French principality of that name. Approaches were made to William, who was married to one of James' daughters. It was hoped he would deliver England from popery.

William had come to prominence in 1672 when France attacked the Dutch Republic, a collection of independent provinces. He led the resistance against his French arch enemy, Louis XIV. A peace agreement was signed in 1678, to the advantage of the Dutch, who had managed to reverse the earlier victories of the French. When James II came to the throne of England William was already married to his daughter, Princess

Mary. A Catholic on the English throne presented the danger of an alliance with Catholic France. Louis was persecuting Huguenots, French Protestants, many of whom fled France to avoid enforced conversion to Catholicism. William began to emerge as the protector of Protestantism in Europe.

In 1688, William decided it would be necessary to invade England as a pre-emptive strike against an inevitable Anglo-French alliance. England was in turmoil. William and his army landed on the south coast of England on 5 November 1688. James, whose army – some 20,000 men – was larger than William's, resolved to fight but then lost his nerve. Anti-Catholic riots erupted in London, soldiers and officers deserted James, rumours spread that he was bringing in French or Irish troops to massacre Protestant subjects. He was in a deep depression, yet would not negotiate with his adversaries. The king fled to France with his wife and newborn son.

Thomas Uniacke had received the news of Charles' death and James accession with delight. Casks of claret were opened in abundance. The taverns of Youghal rang out with the clanking of pewter mugs as Thomas and his friends celebrated their change of fortune. Thomas had always dreamed of this day: that a Catholic king would be returned to the throne of England; the ravages of the Reformation and King Henry VIII would be put right; political power in Ireland would once again rest with the Catholic Anglo-Irish. Thomas' one regret was that his mother was not alive to see the day – Thomas had buried her ten years earlier.

For the first year of James' reign things changed at a slow pace, though increasing numbers of Protestants began to leave Youghal and the surrounding countryside, a pattern common to the rest of the country. St Mary's, its steeple towering above Youghal, was still in the hands of the established Anglican Church, though its congregation now kept a low profile. The practice of closing the gates during Sunday service had ceased. The Protestant community in Youghal came surreptitiously to Church. It was the stated policy of James to respect the religious wishes of Protestants. Though in Ireland Catholics felt a deep bitterness at what had happened under the Cromwellian regime, and indeed for centuries before. The minister of St Mary's, Gilbert Heathcote, saw attendance fall off as more of his parishioners fled or simply stayed away. Soon Heathcote and his family had to leave also.

For the first time in hundreds of years, the rituals of the Roman Catholic Church were being practised within the walls of St Mary's. And for the first time Thomas Uniacke and his family sat in its pews as a Roman Catholic priest stood at the altar and said the Latin Mass. On Sunday mornings, Thomas could march proudly and righteously along Main Street from the ancestral home with his wife and children. The days of receiving the Eucharist in the dark of night were over. Thomas Uniacke's children would be brought up firmly within the Catholic faith.

During the previous ten years, Thomas Uniacke's children had spent considerable lengths of time at the home of their uncle, Robert Fitzgerald of Lisquinlan, a Protestant. There they received an education and were taught the principles of Protestant belief. Ellinor Uniacke was aware her brother Robert was educating her children against the wishes of their father, and contrary to her own beliefs. Realistically she knew there was no alternative, given the unfavourable status for Catholics. The heir to the Uniacke estates was Thomas junior. He was 13 when his uncle Robert went to England in 1687 to escape the growing persecution of his co-religionists.

Within two years of James coming to the throne the religious and political profile of Irish society had been transformed: most army officers were now Catholics, as were judges. In April 1688 the new Catholic corporation was elected for Youghal. Thomas Uniacke became one of its aldermen. The previous year Ellinor Uniacke had unsuccessfully petitioned the king to give her husband the position of Collector of Customs at Cork. So, his election as alderman had been a significant boost for him. Thomas was not the only Uniacke on the corporation. His younger broker Richard was recorder. John Uniacke, a prosperous merchant, was also an alderman, as were his cousins James and Edmond. Thomas welcomed his brother, John, back to the fold of the Church of Rome. But there were others on the corporation he mistrusted, for example Thomas Vaughan Jnr, who had been appointed a bailiff, as his family had been recipients of forfeited Uniacke lands. But if they had genuinely forsaken the ways of heretics, he told himself he could at least tolerate them. He had no sympathy for Protestants who did not see the error of their ways. Through the years 1686, 1687 and 1688, many were driven from their homes or imprisoned on trumped-up charges.

In Dublin, Protestants faced similar persecution. Mary Uniacke was three years widowed when James came to the throne. A Catholic monarch filled her with anxiety. She was well provided for, but had a young family to bring up. The eldest boy, James, was 14 in 1685. It was intended he would eventually take over his father's legal business, after studying in Trinity College. But shortly after the enthronement of the new monarch, the university became a hotbed of student revolt. Pistols and carbines were smuggled into the college, and rumours spread of a plot to assassinate Tyrconnell. For the first year or two, life in Dublin continued as normal. Civil and military changes were taking place behind the scenes. One visible change was the number of monks and priests seen on the streets, causing great amusement to the Protestant children unaccustomed to seeing such sights. By the beginning of 1688, tensions were rising in the metropolis. For the Protestant population a sense of danger and claustrophobia pervaded the capital.

The rights of Protestants were being eroded by proclamations and legislation. In January 1688, they were ordered to hand in all swords and other arms. Failure to do so could mean death. No more than five Protestants could assemble at any one time. A curfew was imposed from 10 o'clock at night until morning. The Church of Ireland archbishop of Dublin, William King, was imprisoned in Dublin Castle. Christ Church cathedral and St Patrick's were taken over by Catholics. Preachers in other Protestant churches in the city were forbidden to speak to their congregation on political matters. The Irish soldiers needed no enticement to desecrate Protestant places of worship. Protestants were forbidden to leave their parishes. Homes were repeatedly searched and ransacked in the search for weapons, young Protestant men were arrested and imprisoned. Protestants were searched as they left Church services.

The recruitment of a Catholic army meant crowds of brawling Irish soldiers drinking in the taverns, chasing whores, and intimidating the Protestant population. Dressed in red coats and black caps the uncouth rural Irish, many with little or no English, took great pleasure in the power they had over the section of the population that had once been their masters. They were billeted with Protestant families, who faced severe retribution if they refused to take them in. Every morning the troops assembled in the streets and then marched away in a motley fashion. They would return in the evening to be fed. In the night the sound of shillelaghs and bodhráns would come from the rooms where the men gathered to smoke their clay pipes and drink whiskey.

Mary Uniacke knew that one day James would be seen as a Protestant man, not a boy, and be shot or imprisoned. He would have to leave Dublin, for the sanctuary of Protestant-controlled Ulster. Ulster, being predominantly Protestant, was able to resist the pressures of King James and the earl of Tyrconnell. In December 1688, the Protestants of Derry closed the gates of the city against an approaching force of James' army led by the Catholic, Lord Antrim. The Catholic population and clergy were forced to leave. A long siege ensued, the events of which are still commemorated today as the Siege of Derry. But James' artillery was inadequate to breach the walls. The siege of Derry was a beacon of hope to the Protestants of Ireland, and demoralising for their Catholic opponents. Conditions were appalling for the besieged: many were dying and dysentery was rife. To survive, the inhabitants were eating dogs, cats, mice and rats – and even tallow. Fresh water was also in short supply. But the morale of James' soldiers was very poor: appalling weather left their camps waterlogged. The army was ill-prepared for a long-term siege. When ships sent by William got through to Derry in July 1689 the spirit of the besieging army was crushed. The siege was broken.

Another centre of Protestant resistance in Ulster was Enniskillen, Co. Fermanagh. From the town, located on the shores of Lough Erne, the cavalry of the Inniskilling regiment led by the Williamite commander Gustavus Hamilton harried the Jacobite forces in the area. By mid 1689, this Protestant army consisted of eight regiments of horse, dragoons and infantry. About this time young James Uniacke enlisted as a junior officer in one of the dragoon regiments, commanded by Sir Albert Conyngham.

James II landed in Ireland in March 1689, at the quaint fishing town of Kinsale, a short distance from Cork city. He arrived in Dublin on Palm Sunday, 24 March to a tumultuous welcome. The Protestant population stayed indoors with the shutters closed. Families played cards or read, candlelight creating some artificial light in their homes. The sounds of harps and singing carried through the narrow streets. Crowds cheered as their monarch approached the city gates. Church bells peeled and cannons fired. There was a growing sense of unease among Protestants, however. And there were reasons to worry: it was unsafe for a Protestant to walk the streets, without being abused and assaulted. Increasingly men were being arrested and imprisoned. Had James Uniacke stayed any longer he would almost certainly have ended up in New Gate gaol or one of the other temporary prisons such as Trinity College, or worse – murdered. For days, the arrival of the king had been expected. News had spread that James II had landed on the south coast and was marching on Dublin with an army of Irish and French soldiers. The rumours were confirmed when labourers were seen putting down fresh gravel on the streets, and Catholic households began hanging flowers and buntings from windows.

Dublin became one mass celebration for the Catholic population on the arrival of their new king. Ireland was the only remaining loyal part of James' former realm, and the stepping-stone to retake the throne of England. The guns of Dublin Castle fired constantly, bonfires were lit, and fireworks exploded and lit up the night sky.

10

'The Pretend Parliament'

Thomas Uniacke was elected as one of the new members of parliament representing the borough of Youghal, along with his friend, Edward Gough. Tyrconnell ensured it would be overwhelmingly Catholic. When he issued the writs summoning parliament he also sent the names of those he wanted to represent each borough. Tyrconnell had obviously favourable accounts of aldermen Uniacke and Gough, and picked them to represent their town. This was perhaps the greatest personal achievement for Thomas Uniacke esquire: when the mayor, Thomas Ronane, summoned the candidate to his chambers in the tholsel one day in late April 1689, to inform him of the summons to attend parliament. He was once again part of the establishment, a ruling class that his ancestors helped to create when it conquered Ireland in the twelfth century.

The parliament met a few weeks later, on 7 May, by which time Thomas would have been well settled at his lodgings. The parliament sat at King's Inns, not the usual Chichester House near Trinity College. King's Inns must have brought back memories for Thomas, which was where the court of claims sat. It had been a less dignified time, when he had to come cap-in-hand begging for what was rightfully his; now carriages lined up outside and the new parliamentarians stepped out. Over 200 members had gathered, from both traditions of Irish life. There were remnants of the old Gaelic families who had ruled before the English – names such as O'Kelly, O'Brien, McNamara and O'Reilly. Then there were the Old English: Fitzgerald, Dillon, Nugent (and of course Uniacke). The latter group held the majority of seats. Gaelic power was a waning tradition. Two of

James' leading Irish generals were elected, Patrick Sarsfield and Justin McCarthy.

The parliament sat on the long benches in the assembly hall awaiting their monarch. Then through the ornately carved doors, to a fanfare of trumpets, strode King James II of England and Ireland, as he was titled. His glinting crown had been specially made in Dublin for the ceremony. But he was king in name only. His rival William had been crowned king of England in February 1689, a jurisdiction that also extended to the Irish parliament. The king rose before his subjects and delivered his controversial speech:

> *I have always been for liberty of conscience and against invading any man's property ... I shall also most readily consent to the making such good and wholesome laws as may be for the general good of the nation, the improvement of trade and the relieving of such as have been injured by the late acts of settlement as far as may be constant with reason, justice and the public good of my people ... And as I shall do my part to make you happy and rich, I make no doubt of your assistance, by enabling me to oppose the unjust designs of my enemies and to make this nation flourish ... I shall conclude as I have begun, and assure you I am as sensible as you can desire of the signal loyalty you have expressed to me, and shall make it my chief study (as it always has been) to make you and all my subjects happy.*

The sitting of this parliament, which came to be called 'The Patriot Parliament', was at times a stormy affair. The king refused to repeal Poyning's Law, which dated back to the fourteenth century and outlawed the Irish parliament from passing legislation without the approval of the English parliament. Thomas Uniacke was not in favour of having two parliaments. Furthermore, he felt no natural affinity with his Gaelic fellow Catholics. They came from a barbaric ancient Celtic world. He did not understand what he saw as a primeval, pagan, dark past. Other contentious issues were the Acts of Settlement and Explanation. The first act went part of the way to returning confiscated Catholic lands, but many families' cases were not resolved. The Act of Explanation rowed back the tide of decrees of innocence by ruling that Protestant grantees would have to return only one-third of their estates. Once again, Thomas was indifferent, being of Old English stock he had regained all his lands. Many of the Catholic landowners were opposed to repealing the acts. Many, such as Tyrconnell, had already bought lands from grantees.

Thomas found the procedures of parliamentary life a bit tiresome. The bill to reverse the land settlement was introduced on 10 May. Three days later, it went to the House of Lords. The amended bill proposed only half the land in question should be returned to Catholics. The Commons rejected the amendment. During the hot clammy summer days tempers became frayed, as the two houses fought it out. Tension was only defused when the welcome, though false, news was announced to the assembly that Derry had surrendered. In the misplaced jubilance that followed, the differences were temporarily forgotten.

Eventually the majority in the Commons got its way by threatening to withhold supplies for James' army. Royal assent was granted on 22 June. A court of claims was to be set up to adjudicate. Catholics who might lose out would be compensated with lands from Williamite supporters.

One bill introduced by the king was warmly received – the Act of Attainder. It referred to the 'most horrid of the king's unnatural enemy, the Prince of Orange, assisted by many of his majesty's rebellious and traitorous subjects.' There were 2,000 Protestant names on the attainder list and if found guilty of treason the penalty would be death and confiscation of lands.

The Catholic Church hierarchy wanted the Act of Uniformity repealed (this recognised Protestantism as the state religion). It also demanded that all restrictive laws be removed and that confiscated Church properties be returned. This was something Thomas had strong opinions on. While he had listened with great pride to his king's opening speech at parliament, and its talk of liberty of conscience, he would soon be a disillusioned man. By the time parliament ended he realised that Catholicism would never have the status it once had. King James wanted to retain the established Protestant Church, fearful of further alienating English Protestants. That he summoned Anglican, and not Catholic, bishops to sit in parliament was an indication of his position.

Sir Richard Nagle, who came from a prominent Cork family and was an alderman on Youghal corporation, was elected speaker. The Uniackes would have known him well. Nagle was also James' attorney general for Ireland and considered a person of high character and a tireless champion for the rights of Catholics. He came from an old Anglo-Irish family, and had earned an excellent reputation at the bar. Educated by the Jesuits he had originally intended to become a priest. It did not take the Members of Parliament long to decide on Sir Richard Nagle, judged by far to be the most distinguished individual, to hold the position.

The parliament sat until 20 July, by which time many members had become disillusioned. The Act of Settlement had been repealed under extreme pressure. On a practical level, parliament had agreed to allocate £20,000 a month for 13 months to help the war effort. But little was done to improve the position of the Church of Rome, which deeply disappointed Thomas Uniacke. He did not know that the whole pageant had been pretence and within a year events on the battlefield had shattered all the enactments and dreams of the Patriots' Parliament. The tide of history had not been turned – it was still ebbing and flowing.

11

Battle of the Boyne

In the autumn of 1689, William of Orange dispatched one of his most senior generals, the duke of Schomberg, to Ireland. Landing in Belfast, Schomberg quickly moved to take the port of Carrickfergus after a week-long siege of its castle. He then moved south towards Dublin, through countryside devastated by retreating Jacobite forces. Towards the end of the year the Williamite force was nearing the capital. But Schomberg needed to get his army into winter quarters. Furthermore, he was losing large numbers of soldiers to illnesses such as dysentery.

The winter of 1689–90 was exceptionally cold, the spring exceptionally wet. By now, William was convinced that his own presence in Ireland was necessary if the campaign was to be successful; privately he was unhappy with the progress Schomberg was making. William was determined to conclude his war against James II in Ireland, and was keen to get back to the continent and continue his war against the French. Ireland was merely a sideshow, to put an end to the threat posed by his father-in-law. William landed in Carrickfergus in June 1690 with further reinforcements. By the end of that month, the two armies were inching closer to the decisive battle. William's force of 35,000 men – with a large continental contingent – was moving south along the east coast while James' army, with 26,000 soldiers, was marching northwards from Dublin. James finally decided that the river Boyne in Co. Meath was to be the line of defence. This was where he would defend the capital – he believed if he lost Dublin, he would have lost the country.

King James assembled his men near the village of Oldbridge on the south bank, which was one of the few places that the Boyne could be easily crossed. It was two miles upstream from

Drogheda. By the morning of 30 June, he was positioned on the hill of Donore, overlooking the village. On the opposite side stretched open fields, copses and hedgerows. Peaceful in the lush green of summer, the twittering of the birds gave no indication of the blood that would soon flow. The green river meandered gently, its still surface mirroring the trees and rushes by its banks. Naturally, no work was being done in the fields. The only sound was the soldiers who had occupied Oldbridge, as they dug trenches and made loopholes in the walls of the houses. The inhabitants of the village had fled. All of James' troops were now massed on the south side. They watched the northern horizon that sloped down to the riverbank for sight of the enemy, which their scouts reported would arrive very shortly.

Then, by mid-morning, Jacobite soldiers scanning the opposite ridge from Donore, saw figures appear on the skyline. More and more – foot and cavalry – began to appear. Gradually they moved down the hillside, where they began to pitch their tents. Soon white tents stretched across the undulating countryside. Soldiers sat in the ploughed fields and meadows and among the trees awaiting orders. Just before noon, they were mustered. The Jacobites had been watching them intently, and braced themselves when they heard the drum call. Through their glasses, they could make out William ride along the ridge top. His army was now lined up on the slopes in battle formation. The order was sounded for the columns to move down. As they edged nearer, the Jacobites readied themselves, should any attempt be made to cross.

For a year, James Uniacke had trained in the opposing camp: how to use a carbine and pistol, fight with a sword, handle a horse in battle but now he was on the threshold of his first battle and facing the very real possibility of death. As a cornet in the Inniskilling Dragoons, he was in charge of a unit of horsemen even though some of them must have been older than himself.

The Inniskilling Dragoons formed a long line across a plough-ed field. They were lined up with other cavalry regiments, and within range of the enemy guns.

But then a bugle ordered their retreat. William wouldn't go into battle that day. It was a Monday, and William of Orange was superstitious about fighting on Mondays, believing it brought bad luck. The troops returned to the camp at Tullyallen, about two miles from the Boyne. Then about three o'clock William was seen riding towards the river. It caused a stir of interest and broke the boredom. He had several of his officers with him. No-body had any idea what was happening. Less than an hour later, the sound of two cannon rounds peeled its way back to the camp, causing a flurry. Shortly afterwards their king returned, but he was slumped on his horse, and his face was a deathly pale. A white bloodstained cloth covered his right shoulder. He was helped off his horse and led into his tent. The news was quickly passed on that the king had only been grazed and was in no dan-ger. The soldiers and officers wanted to know what happened. Soon the truth came filtering through.

William had led his officers to the riverbank under the sus-picious and watchful eye of the enemy. Then he decided to stop in a glen that ran down to the water's edge. There he and his men had a picnic – to the complete amazement of the Jacobites. Under cover of the hedgerows, they brought small cannons as close to William as possible. They were not going to turn down an opportunity to assassinate King William of Orange himself. He was lucky to escape with the injuries he did.

That evening William was strong enough to call his council of war, where the plans for the next day's fighting were decided. Of course, none of the men, except for the most senior officers, had any idea what was going to happen. A feverish impatience spread through the camp: all they wanted now was the chance to meet the popish enemy face to face and as the last rays of angled sunlight pierced through the Williamite camp the army settled down to an uneasy sleep.

At 2a.m. on 1 July 1690, the camp was woken as men started to assemble. A party of cavalry, infantry and dragoons was
preparing to move out. Count Schomberg, son of the duke of
Schomberg, William's military commander, was to lead some
10,000 men westward to find another suitable crossing point. At
5a.m., the drums began to roll and the detachment marched out.
A dense grey mist covered the countryside, reducing visibility to
a few feet. On the other side of the river the Jacobite camp was
alerted by the sound of the drums. But they could see little further than the lower slopes of the north bank. They readied
themselves for a frontal attack at Oldbridge.

In the dim light, the Inniskillingers prepared themselves:
horses were watered, fed, and groomed. The cavalrymen checked their equipment. Each Inniskillinger was armed with a fire-
lock musket and two pistols, the first carried in a bucket on the
flap of the saddle, the pistols placed on either side of the pom-
mel of the saddle. A goatskin was strapped over the holsters to
protect them from the weather. The men checked their ammunition and then placed it in the cartouche box on the right side.
Finally, they put on their broadsword and bayonet. Mounting
their horses, the dragoons, in the iron-grey colour uniforms, fell
into line and awaited their orders.

Count Schomberg chose Rosnaree, two miles away, as the
best point to attempt a crossing. The land was still shrouded in
mist when the attack commenced. James Uniacke was lined up
for inspection when they heard the rumble of cannon fire. Schomberg's men were coming under attack. From a steep hill opposite,
Sir Neil O'Neill's regiment of dragoons was in waiting, along
with five artillery pieces, now pounding away. Williamite grenadiers and dragoons were the first across. Superior numbers forced
the Jacobites to fall back. O'Neill was wounded and died later.

The Jacobite command was in some confusion. They had
heard the drums beat as the first Williamite detachment decamped, but were unable to see anything because of the mist.

Shortly after six, William sent General Douglas with infantry and a brigade of cavalry to Rosnaree to back up Schomberg. By then, the sun was burning away the mist, and the columns of moving men were visible. An animated discussion was taking place between James II and his generals. The intelligence was confused, James had reports that the enemy had taken the bridge at Slane, and not that they had crossed at Rosnaree. Lauzun, the commander of the French army fighting with the Irish, agreed with James that the main attack was taking place further west. The Jacobites wanted to move the bulk of their army caught in the bend of the river as they felt they could find themselves encircled. The French general, la Hoguette, disagreed, saying that the defences at Oldbridge should not be weakened but he was over-ruled.

Soon Jacobites were raising their tents and marching west. From the northern slopes of the Boyne William trained his telescope along the slopes and hilltops and saw clearly what was happening. James was moving west with the bulk of his army to meet the challenge from William's 'main force' at Rosnaree. He was wrong, William was keeping his main thrust for Oldbridge. Two regiments of Jacobite cavalry, a large percentage of the Irish infantry, and all six French foot battalions went to the aid of their comrades. Some 6,000 soldiers remained at Oldbridge: to face an enemy of over 20,000.

The battle at Rosnaree was making little progress. About 10,000 Williamites had crossed and were in command of the steep slope. They could see the approaching Jacobite reinforcements by the huge cloud of dust raised. They could hear the whistle of their own cannon targeting the moving army. But the terrain at Rosnaree made a further encounter difficult. Boggy ground and ditches with steep banks divided the armies. This made a cavalry charge virtually impossible.

By nine o'clock, there was not a single cloud in the sky, and the heat was intense. The Inniskillingers were positioned at

Drybridge, about half a mile downstream from Oldbridge. The village was in clear view, and appeared deserted. Then the artillery to the right of the dragoons began to pound the village. Out of sight, in the ravine where William had picnicked the previous afternoon, the Dutch Blue Guards were assembling. At ten, when the river was at low tide, the guards began to beat a march and moved out of the ravine towards the bank. Then the drums ceased. Ten abreast the guards waded into the river, the water rising to their chests. When halfway across, Oldbridge came to life: musketeers firing from the hedges, breastworks, houses and yards. Guards stumbled and fell.

Like everyone else James Uniacke watched anxiously as the Dutch attempted to make a bridgehead against a wall of fire. First across were the grenadiers, who with their grenades made the Jacobite infantry retreat. But then waves of cavalry descended on the guards from behind the hilltop. They seemed to appear from nowhere. Plumes of smoke and sparks of flying shrapnel grounded some of the men and horses, but still they fell upon the guards. Having gained sufficient foothold the guards started firing volley after volley at the enemy. Then they screwed their bayonets into their muskets to meet a further onslaught, while flanking platoons gave them cover. This forced the Jacobites back, though they kept charging repeatedly. By now the Blue Guards regiment was across, followed by Huguenot and English regiments of foot. Sheer numbers meant the Jacobites were unable to prevent a bridgehead being established. In Oldbridge, along the banks and on the slopes, the fiercest of the fighting took place. About 150 Irish and 100 Dutch Blue Guards were killed. Included among the dead was the duke of Schomberg, shot in the throat.

William then ordered a further 12,000 English and Danish troops across, just downstream from Oldbridge. By now, masses of Williamites were wading, swimming and scrambling across the Boyne. The Jacobites were being spread too thinly to be able to repulse them. A whole melee of noises reached the Inniskillingers – musket shot, cannon fire, clashing swords, screams and shouts, neighing horses. At noon, William rode to the front of the detachment overlooking Drybridge. Wearing the royal star and garter he was conspicuous to the enemy. But, in spite of being wounded the previous day, the Protestant king was unfazed. His bravery was indisputable. He addressed himself to the cavalrymen of Conynham's regiment, who were to lead the third crossing of the river. 'Gentlemen, I have heard much of your exploits and now I shall witness them.'

Placing himself at the front, he led the Inniskillingers into battle. With a deafening thunder of hooves, they galloped down the hill and through the river. The king's horse floundered on the south bank. William was helped off while a soldier pulled the animal out of the boggy ground. The dragoons fanned out around him. Jacobite musketeers were firing, the pellets peppering the surface of the river. King William was sitting on the bank breathing with difficulty. His face was pale as porcelain. The bank was only thinly defended so William was a clear target to any musketeer. At that moment Jacobite dragoons charged from the thicket on to the flatter boggy ground. Inniskillingers came forward to meet them.

James Uniacke put his training into practice, firing his musket and pistols, and then drawing out his sword. Within a few moments, William was once again leading his army, throwing himself into the fray. Soon the Jacobites were in retreat. But they rallied several times before giving up the ghost. The cavalry, particularly the young English Jacobite, Major General Dominic Sheldon's Irish Horse, distinguished itself with its bravery.

The Williamites were inching their way up the southern slopes towards Donore Hill. But the Irish were not giving up the hill easily. The fighting was becoming confused. Some Inniskillingers mistook the Dutch guard for Irish. William was now leading the Dutch troops when a group of Inniskillingers appeared from the other side of the hill. They charged the Dutch, who were almost scattered. William waved his sword, calling his men to order. One Inniskillinger pointed his pistol at William, who replied: 'Are you angry with your friends?' William had a number of lucky escapes: later a bullet hit his boot. The first attempt to take Donore was unsuccessful. But after a recharge, the Jacobite line was broken.

The Irish infantry, badly equipped and poorly trained, fled the battlefield, leaving their baggage as booty for the victors – some even dropped their weapons. The cavalry tried to hold up the Williamites for as long as possible. As William's cavalry was regrouping Sheldon's Irish Horse made another charge from Plattin Hill, just to the south of Donore Hill. They engaged the Dutch guard furiously, but were finally driven back.

Meanwhile at Rosnaree, James II was facing William's right flank across the rough impassable terrain. James and Lauzun were discussing tactics when an aide-de-camp rode up with the news – the right wing had been broken, the enemy had forded the river at Oldbridge. An intense argument followed: la Hoguette said the ground at Rosnaree could be traversed, but James and Lauzun were more concerned with being encircled. They ruled out charging the enemy facing them – the only chance of changing the course of the battle.

La Hoguette was proved right. Shortly afterwards some of General Douglas' dragoons ploughed straight through the bog that separated the two armies. With William moving south from Donore, James felt trapped. He could see the dust being raised by the Williamite horse, heading for the Dublin road. James ordered the retreat, climbed aboard his royal carriage and sped towards Duleek, situated on the river Nanny. If William's men got there first there would be no escape. Lauzun ordered his carriage to be readied, and his infantry and horsemen to move out.

The scene at Duleek was chaotic. The locals cowered in the cottages and huts of the muddy one-street town. From before mid-afternoon bedraggled soldiers started passing through, some stealing horses for the journey, other demanding water and food. But most just kept running. Soon the trickle grew to torrent. Both parts of James' army collided at Duleek's bridge. One of the foot regiments, marching in a orderly fashion, was suddenly scattered as it made its way down a high banked lane: some of their own horsemen galloped through them firing pistols to clear the way. The infantrymen took to their heels. The duke of Berwick, James' illegitimate son, almost ordered his musketeers to fire on his own horsemen, thinking them Williamites.

Amid all this confusion, James II's carriage crossed the narrow bridge. The sound of gunfire could be heard above all the noise. Just north of Duleek, the French cavalry were engaging the enemy, the only action the French saw that day. It managed to hold up the attackers, who had been chasing the Irish from hilltop to hilltop through the afternoon. King James was advised to head for Dublin as fast as possible: Williamite cavalry and dragoons were not far behind, and could even make it there before him.

By 8 o'clock that evening James Uniacke and his men were back at Oldbridge. The cornet had survived death, and had killed men for the first time. Around him was the landscape of carnage. The fields were puckered with scorched craters. Dead men and horses littered the fields and clung to the bulrushes by the river. Baggage, clothes and weapons lay about. Flames and smoke rose from Oldbridge. In the twilight, women and children were still stripping down the bodies, rooting through baggage on the grass. Others had already made off with plate and money discovered in abandoned wagons. But James Uniacke would live to see another day.

About 9 o'clock, Mary Uniacke heard the sound of a carriage going through the streets at high speed. It was King James heading towards Dublin Castle. As the hoofs and wheels clattered over the timbers of the drawbridge into the castle, silence descended again. Rumours abounded from about teatime that the Jacobites had been defeated and shortly afterwards soldiers appearing in the outskirts seemed to confirm this. As dusk fell, an uneasy silence settled on the city and fears spread that the remaining Jacobite army might close the gates and take the Protestant population hostage.

Just before dawn the next morning, Mary Uniacke heard the faint sound of horses and voices. In those early silent hours, any sound would carry through the narrow streets of the city. She did not know it, but the sounds were coming from the castle courtyard, where James II and his entourage were preparing to leave. She heard them move through the streets and out into the country, fading away. This was a worrying time for the widow. She fretted for her son: was he lying on the battlefield dead? Was he injured and suffering great agony?

On departing Dublin James II headed for Duncannon near Waterford, where he set sail for France. As Ireland disappeared on the horizon so did his dream of ever regaining his crown.

On the northern outskirts of Dublin the last of the Jacobites were gathering in the meadows, and regrouping into their old regiments. But they would not take the city. Instead they were ordered to march west, to Limerick and the natural boundaries of the Shannon river. There they would make their final stand. The news that the papists had given up Dublin quickly spread. That night a festive mood filled the Uniacke household, like every relieved Protestant household. At least they were safe. But they heard cries and breaking glass – Protestants were now taking vengeance against the Catholic population.

On 6 July, William sent a troop of Dutch guards to take control of the capital. How smart they looked in their blue uniforms as they rode in. The church bells rang out and bunting hung from houses and shops. It was reminiscent of when James II had entered, but then Protestants remained indoors. Crowds cheered in the streets. If Mary Uniacke brought her children to the square in front of Dublin Castle to see the spectacle, in the hope of glimpsing her son, she would have been disappointed. It would be a few days before James would get leave to visit his family. But his stay would not be long – for Ireland's fate had yet to be decided.

12

The Aftermath

The Jacobite defeat came as a blow to Thomas Uniacke. As soon as the news reached Youghal, the town mayor, Thomas Ronayne, called a meeting of all the aldermen to discuss developments. The latest was that William had taken Dublin and the Irish had retreated to Limerick, along with a force of French troops. Resistance seemed pointless. William's victorious army was sweeping south and westwards towards the Shannon. As July progressed, news of the surrenders of Wexford, Waterford and Duncannon arrived in Youghal. Most Jacobite forces in the area had gone. On 2 August, Youghal surrendered to William's authority when a force of 50 dragoons from Colonel Levison's regiment rode up to the town walls. Smoke rose from the chimneys of the tholsel as officials destroyed all the documents related to the short life of that Catholic corporation.

Youghal was of strategic importance for launching an attack on the Catholic garrison in Cork city and curbing the activities of Irish rapparees in the eastern part of the county. On 9 August, a force of 36 dragoons and over 40 foot-soldiers marched towards Castlemartyr to engage a party of Irish rebels. In Youghal tensions remained high; uncertainty created anxiety. What would the new Protestant authorities do? Catholics feared revenge would be a high priority. Rumours of atrocities spread. Whether true or not, they instilled terror.

Cork city had strong defences and would be hard to defeat, argued Thomas when in hushed conversation with fellow Catholics. But the southern port fell to an efficient three-week campaign commanded by John Churchill, the later earl of Marlborough. A large force – 5,000 in total and including marines –

was rumoured to have landed at the mouth of Cork harbour. The governor of the city, Colonel Roger MacElligott was determined to resist. He was an experienced officer with some 4,000 troops.

Life around Youghal went on as normal as the battle for Cork raged, not twenty miles away. All the hay had been gathered in, to see the animals through yet another uncertain winter. On 27 September, the town heard news of Cork's surrender. The bombardment of Cork from the high ground overlooking the city had soon breached the wall and the Jacobite outworks were overrun. The defenders were short of ammunition and facing certain defeat. MacElligott surrendered and the garrison was made prisoners of war. Other Jacobite forces could not come to the rescue of Cork, as preparing for the coming winter became more urgent. After Cork Marlborough attacked Kinsale – it soon capitulated.

From early August, the Williamites were encamped outside Limerick. The bombardment of the city walls was making little impression, despite William's confidence it would soon fall. This was a view shared by the French, who had deserted Limerick for Galway on the western seaboard, believing it could not withstand a siege. The Irish were left to defend it on their own. Limerick was divided in two parts: English Town and Irish Town. The old English quarter was on an island in the river Shannon, linked by a bridge to the Irish Town on the southern bank. William's forces were located to the south-east of the walls, while the Irish still had access to the north bank in Co. Clare, via Thomond Bridge.

The hot dry summer was giving way to a wet autumn. Young James Uniacke was spending a lot of time in his tent, the rain pelting against the canvas and gusts of wind carrying drops of water through the flaps. The ground within the tents was soggy and damp – outside feet just sank into the mud. Some of the trenches had become virtual pools. Morale among the troops was at an all-time low. Not even the flamboyant heroism of their king was enough to raise their spirits. One morning he rode out with some of his officers to inspect a weak point in the walls. Someone stopped him for a word: at that very moment a cannon ball whizzed past him. Had he not stopped it would have blown him to pieces. Even his tent was said to be in range of Irish bullets.

There was a further blow to Williamite morale, and one that seriously hampered the military operation. A daring Irish cavalry officer, Patrick Sarsfield, attacked the siege train on the way to Limerick. It consisted of eight pieces of large artillery, powder, tools and small bridge boats. There were about 100 wagons and carts, most of which were destroyed. On 27 August, out of frustration, William ordered an attack. The troops were to storm a breach made in part of the wall. But the operation was a disaster. The Inniskillingers held back as the earl of Drogheda's grenadiers entered the breach, and started making their way along the narrow streets. The shots echoed loudly in the pouring rain. The screams and clash of swords rang out. The trumpet sounded for the dragoons to charge. James Uniacke galloped across the waterlogged fields towards the walls. But the Irish were pushing the grenadiers back. When the Inniskillingers reached the breach they came under a massive barrage: from the walls the Irish began throwing grenades down on them. They exploded round the horsemen like claps of thunder. James and his troop fired their carbines at the ramparts, but to little effect.

Even the women of Limerick joined in the fight, flinging bottles and stones at the enemy. When James and his men managed to enter the breach, they found themselves in a narrow laneway, stacked high with corpses and wounded. The injured men howled and groaned as they lay in pools of their own blood. Further down, Drogheda's men were battling with the Irish. A cloud of smoke from muskets and pistols hung in the air.

After three hours of fighting in dark lanes and alleys the Williamites had to retreat. The Inniskillingers held back the

Irish while the injured were helped out. Finally, they made their exit, missiles falling on them from the walls. James had witnessed the devastating effect of grenades exploding over men's heads: on the ground lay their victims, skulls blasted open, exposing brains and blood to the elements. Back in the camp the soldiers watched as the Irish flung the corpses over the walls and out of the breach. Many looked intact and unblemished as if they were asleep, others were missing heads or limbs. The unattached body parts were thrown out after them.

Next morning James was woken before dawn by the noise of the rain on the roof of his tent. He did not know yet, but that was the last day he would spend outside Limerick, until the following year at least. On Friday 28 August the Williamite army decamped, leaving behind the boggy marshes and the winds that gusted up the Shannon from the Atlantic; and of course their dead comrades, now left to be devoured by the crows and the rats.

After the surrender of Cork, Thomas Uniacke became more despondent as chilling accounts of the treatment of the population began to filter out. Houses were looted and burned in the initial days. Catholics were forcibly moved to the East Marsh outside the city. By the beginning of October, there were accounts of numerous deaths from starvation and sickness. In comparison, Youghal had remained untouched: life went on as normal, Catholics were not molested. But, as during the reign of Cromwell, their fate lay in the hands of others.

The Williamite army began attacking Jacobite strongholds in Kerry, as the county was an important source of supplies for Limerick. There was one glimmer of hope that raised Thomas Uniacke's spirits – the exploits of Patrick Sarsfield. He was the rising hero of the Jacobite cause. The young gallant cavalry officer was the one popular hope of driving King William out of Ireland. Pamphlets reported his attack on the siege train in August and how daringly he had taken the initiative. Having received intelligence from a Williamite deserter, he crossed the river Shannon from Co. Clare with a crack force of cavalrymen and dragoons. The train had stopped at a place called Ballyneety, only ten miles from William's camp, and the guard thought they were safe. They had travelled from Dublin, through the boggy wilderness of the midlands, at all times in danger of guerrilla attack. On the last evening of their journey, they put their horses into the fields, and settled down for a peaceful night.

Sarsfield, with some 500 men, attacked them at about two in the morning. The guards were quickly overpowered, and either fled or were killed. The exploding powder lighted up the night sky. It was a devastating success – all the powder and guns were destroyed, wagons set ablaze, supplies of corn destroyed. The boats that were to ferry soldiers across the Shannon were holed. Some 60 people were killed. The resulting explosion had blown large chunks of the artillery pieces, and bodies, into the surrounding fields.

Sarsfield was the nearest thing to the embodiment of Old English Catholic nobility in Ireland, in Thomas' opinion. All classes of Irishmen supported him. Like the Uniackes, he was of Old Anglo-Irish stock; the first Sarsfields had come to Ireland in 1172 as standard bearers for Henry II. Patrick Sarsfield's great-great grandfather, Sir William, was knighted in 1566 for his part in suppressing Shane O'Neill's rebellion.

Stories abounded that a man called Galloping Hogan, a local rapparee, had guided Sarsfield through the countryside on his night ride. He knew every 'track and roadway, every ford and bog'. With his help the bold Sarsfield was able to elude the English forces that he was sure were searching for him. The peaceful August landscape was illuminated by a harvest moon, lighting up a silvery path.

A sympathiser in the English camp had passed on the password – which quickly got back to the enemy, so the story goes. Ironically, the password was 'Sarsfield', and when Sarsfield descended on the camp, he called out to the sentry: 'Sarsfield is the word'. And as his cavalrymen rushed the English he added: 'Sarsfield is the man'. The unsuspecting enemy was awoken to the noise of trampling hooves. They attempted to get their horses but were cut down. The commander, Thomas Poultney, fumbled to get his boots on as the Irish swept between the tents and wagons firing their carbines and lashing with their sabres. Many of the English fled to the nearby wood so fearful was the pande-monium. Sarsfield and his men disappeared into the night – their work done – leaving the burning skyline behind them.

Further rumours spread throughout the country: in Cork the Jacobite Colonel MacElligott was leading a force of 8,000 men, and 'ranging' across the south of Ireland. A force of 3,000 led by Berwick and Sheldon was planning an attack on Dublin. Bands of Irish troops were burning towns in every part of Ireland. For a brief interval, the English were becoming worried.

There were skirmishes over the winter. Just after Christmas 1,500 Irish attacked the Danish garrison at Fermoy in north Co. Cork, but were driven away. Rapparees burnt down Protestant farmsteads in rural areas. Williamite forces plundered Catholic homes. In March, rumours reached Youghal that Sarsfield was planning to lead an attack on the pass at Fermoy. Reinforce-ments were sent to protect it. But the attack never materialised. Later that month 15 rapparees were hanged at Clonmel in Co. Tipperary.

James Uniacke saw little action throughout the winter, and was quartered in Enniskillen for most of it. Because of the state of the country, he was unable to visit his family in Dublin for Christmas as it would have been too dangerous. To be caught by Irish rebels would mean a hideous and painful death. By June, he was ready to play his part in finishing off the war against popery. On 18 June, the army of King William, led by Ginkel, opened the summer season with an attack on Athlone in the midlands. The 25,000 strong force comprised 30 infantry battalions, 40 horse and dragoon squadrons, over 30 siege guns, 6 mortars and 12 field guns. It massed on the eastern banks of the Shannon. On the far side were the Jacobites, now under the command of the French general, Marquis de St Ruth. Athlone was the gateway to Connaught. The town stretched across both banks, connected by a stone bridge.

Ginkel's guns started firing on the morning of 20 June. By nightfall, they had forced the Irish across the bridge into the western half of Athlone. When darkness fell, a red glow lit up the sky as buildings burned, the sound of collapsing timbers and smell of charcoal filled the air. The Jacobites fled across the bridge under musket fire, bravely managing to break two of the nine arches. For several days Ginkel bombed the western bank and sent waves of troops to try to capture the bridge. But the small force of Irish was mounting an impressive defence. On 29 June, the Williamites edged their way to the centre of the bridge, where they had earlier managed to cross the chasm with planks. But the brushwood fascines and covering gallery, which gave protection against grenades and musketry, were set on fire. The attackers had to retreat. But a surprise attack the following evening brought about the capture of Athlone. A storming party was led by Major General Hugh Mackay, while a German officer in the Danish army, Major General Tettau, led another unit across the river. His troops waded through the river just below the arches of the bridge, grenadiers in front, and were quickly in the town. Soon a 2,000-strong attacking force of Ginkel's best units, including James Uniacke and the Inniskillingers, were on the other bank. It was all over in half an hour.

For several days the Williamites made their way through a landscape of low hillocks and hazel bush undergrowth. The ground had become waterlogged after days of continuous rain. Thunder and lightning storms were frequent. The hills and scrubland stared at them menacingly. Ginkel did not even know where the enemy was – they could be ambushed at any moment. Scouting parties of cavalry and dragoons, James Uniacke among them, were sent out to locate the Jacobites. This was probably the most terrifying type of warfare: the dragoon could not see the enemy. A cracking twig could be a papist or a harmless animal. Every gully entered could be a trap. Over every hilltop could be the entire enemy army. This made the elite dragoons feral, muscles taut, ready to fight. The senses were sharpened, alert to any sound or sight.

Marquis de St Ruth's army was discovered on Saturday, 11 July. It had taken up a defensive position on a long ridge called Aughrim Hill (also known as Kilcommadan Hill). It stretched south-east from the ruined castle and village of Aughrim to a place called Tristaun. Ginkel's dragoons could see them clearly, dotted along the western skyline. The intelligence was quickly passed back. St Ruth was situated on the eastern slope of the ridge, his left held the old castle, while his right were positioned beside a stream. Facing Aughrim Hill was a bog, divided by a river and beyond that stood Urraghry Hill. The Irish were pro-tected by bog and river. The bog was impassable, but a narrow causeway gave access to the area near the castle. An esker acted as a bridge to the other end of the ridge.

There was a dense fog next morning as the Williamite army was mustered, just as on the morning of the Boyne. Still blan-keted in greyness the army marched out, prepared to do battle. The force advanced in several columns. Each musketeer carried 15 charges, each foot regiment marched with five pioneers in front, and the grenadiers guarded the flanks, their shells at the ready. Outside them rode the dragoons.

By early afternoon the first contact was made with the enemy. Danish advance cavalry met some Jacobite horse just south of Urraghry Hill. An intense skirmish followed. James' regiment was ordered to give support, and was moved from the right side to the left, where the fighting was taking place. The horsemen galloped through rugged countryside of hedges and copses towards the foot of Urraghry Hill. James could now hear the sound of battle over the noise of his own horses. Around one final wall of bracken and they were in the thick of the fighting. They dismounted and waded in but soon the Irish were being pushed back. With the arrival of a further horse regiment the Jacobites finally acceded and made their way along the esker towards Tristaun.

Now in command of Urraghry Hill, the Inniskillingers had a clear view of the enemy. Once they were satisfied the hill was safe, General Ginkel and his staff rode up. The cavalry and dragoons dismounted and rested on the slopes about half a mile away from the enemy. Soon the infantry joined the advance parties as they scrambled up the southern slope. The sky was now clearing. At about 2 o'clock, Williamite cannons started firing, raising clouds of smoke from the slopes of Aughrim Hill. Then, in midafternoon, fresh fighting broke out on the esker, as more waves of Irish went on the offensive. Cunningham's dragoons were ordered in again. Much of the fighting took place near a brook that divided the two armies.

Meanwhile, Ginkel was in conference with his senior officers. Some advised that the army should encamp for the night and launch the battle next morning. But Major General Mackay argued for an immediate attack on both wings of St Ruth's army.

It was about five o'clock in the evening, and the battle was beginning in earnest. As the sun sank lower, the Williamite army went on full scale offensive, advancing on St Ruth's right and left wing. The right side was being pushed back slowly. The Williamites eventually forded the river, aided greatly by their superior artillery power: shots from nine, six and three pounders whistling over their heads. On the opposite side, the Irish dragoons and infantry were waiting, protected by a series of ditches, on marshy ground dotted with hedgerows. Cunningham's dragoons and Portland's regiment of horse, assisted by Eppinger, Ruvigny and Lanier's regiments were now dismounted and fighting hand to hand in the ditches. Further back on the smoother ground stood the Irish horse, which were not to be underestimated following their bravery at the Boyne. The cavalry troops were at something of a disadvantage. The ground near the stream was not ideal for horses – and the Irish in the ditches were holding out well.

There was intense fighting further along the battlefront. A Williamite battery was moved nearer the causeway leading to the castle to cover the whole of Ginkel's right wing as it attempted to cross the causeway. But the causeway was narrow, so some battalions had to advance via the bog just below it. They were out of range of the Jacobite musketeers, but could see the troops lined along the slopes of the ridge. However, the abundance of hedgerows could have concealed many more soldiers. Once within range the Williamites came under heavy musket fire from the hedges and took cover in a line of ditches.

The Williamite cavalry, bravely led by Major General Mackay, eventually made it across the causeway, under fire from the castle and the trenches in front. St Ruth had weakened his left wing by moving forces to the right. The Williamite army in the centre now moved forward. It met the same guerrilla tactics from the Irish infantry. The musketeers were crouched so low behind their ditches the English could not see them. When they were within 20 yards the Irish fired, driving them back. They pursued them, using their muskets as clubs. The 2,000 Williamite foot were in retreat. The Jacobites chased them right across the bog. From Urraghry Hill, Ginkel could see a white flag with a red hand in its centre being placed on one of the Williamite batteries. It had been captured by troops of Gordon O'Neill's Regiment. The symbol represented the red hand of Ulster.

St Ruth rode along the ridge assessing the battle: the tenacious infantry forcing back the enemy on the right, the success of Williamite cavalry on his left flank. Then the path of his horse met that of a cannon ball. The general's head was blown off his shoulders. Confusion descended on the Irish as they saw his corpse, draped in a cloak, being carried from the battlefield. The enemy knew nothing of this.

Mackay's assault on the causeway was the breakthrough the English needed. More infantry battalions came over and soon the fighting had moved on to Aughrim village, a small cluster of cabins. The Irish cavalry was too weak on that side to repulse the Williamites even though the Irish infantry fought stubbornly to prevent more foot advancing from the bog. Around this time, the Irish cavalry deserted the field. Without their support the Irish infantry, who had fought so bravely at Aughrim, had no choice but to flee. They were now being pushed back up the slopes of Aughrim Hill, retreating ditch by ditch. Their right wing, which had been holding the enemy for hours, was collapsing.

Throughout the afternoon, James Uniacke had seen a number of his men wounded and killed. But now the Irish were running. He regrouped his men and ordered them to give chase. The sky was overcast and a misty rain was falling, reducing visibility. In the half-light of dusk, they made their way over the uneven ground and the ditches. Musketeers bayoneted those Irish still lying in the ditches, while the horsemen and dragoons mounted when they got to the dry even ground. The Jacobite infantry headed for the hilltop, the dragoons in chase. When he got close James Uniacke fired his pistol into the back of his running target, finishing him off with his sword should the victim groan or move after falling. Some of the Irish still showed great bravery, the more pugnacious of them turning to fight the oncoming horse. By nine o'clock it was over.

The Williamite army was soon on the march again. First to Galway, which surrendered promptly, and then back to Limerick. By 25 August, they were once again encamped outside the city walls. But it would be another fortnight before the artillery arrived. Tyrconnell, who had masterminded James II's operations in Ireland, had died on 14 August from a stroke and was buried in an unmarked plot in Limerick cathedral. The Irish were desperate: promised supplies from France had not arrived. Jacobite resistance was limited to counties Clare, Kerry and Limerick. They were still a large army, but had few weapons, and there was a shortage of forage for the horses. After Aughrim, morale among the men was at an all-time low.

On 22 September, the Williamites began a determined bombardment of Limerick. This time from west of the Shannon, where they had crossed the river further upstream. The Irish fled across Thomond Bridge only to find the drawbridge had been raised. Apparently, in the confusion, an officer raised it – leaving scores of Irish to be massacred. Yet, the Irish were well fortified within the walls of Limerick. Another winter was approaching and the Williamite commanders were considering putting the campaign on hold for the winter. This would mean the war carrying on into the next year. But the Irish were psychologically defeated: carrying on would simply postpone their defeat.

On 25 September 1691, a delegation of Irish met with Ginkel. From the outset, Ginkel agreed that any of the Irish soldiers who wanted to go to France could do so, but the landowners among them would have their properties forfeited. The Irish would not surrender unconditionally, they demanded a pardon for all Catholics, the restoration of Catholic estates at the time of James II's flight from England, freedom of worship, a priest in every parish, no discrimination in civil or military employment and civil and commercial rights. The negotiators also demanded that the terms of any peace agreement be ratified by parliament. Ginkel rejected these conditions, which would never be accepted by Irish or English Protestants.

After further bargaining, what came to be known as the Treaty of Limerick was signed on 3 October 1691. There were 13 civil articles, and the second was to be the cause of controversy. The Irish had insisted that the article be amended so that the immunity granted to Irish soldiers in the parts of the country controlled by the Jacobites would also apply to the civilian population in these areas. In the final draft the additional clause was omitted, which almost lead to the treaty's collapse. The Williamites assured the Irish that the omission was due to human error, and was not deliberate. King William ordered that the clause be reinserted. Irish Protestants resented the concessions made to the Irish negotiators. Every opportunity to undermine the treaty was seized upon.

So with 25,000 dead and the country devastated by disease and famine, the war ended. On a personal note, James Uniacke had received no news from home for almost a year. He did not know that on 30 April his mother had died. He would not become aware of the tragic news until he returned to Dublin at the end of the war.

The one hope for Ireland, in the opinion of Thomas Uniacke and so many Irish men, was still in the person of Patrick Sarsfield. And when James II had made him earl of Lucan, it confirmed his pedigree. But the dashing earl sailed from the shores of Ireland after the war, to fight in the army of Louis XIV, and to die on a foreign battlefield doing what he did best.

13

The Outlawed

By Michaelmas 1690 retribution against Irish Jacobites had begun. All members of James' Catholic parliament were deemed guilty of high treason, and faced the prospect of being hanged, drawn and quartered. The legal process began with a bill of indictment, followed by the issuing of a warrant by the sheriff. If the accused appeared he was either bound over for another hearing or tried there and then by a judge and jury. If the accused did not appear, after the issuing of a second writ the sheriff issued a writ of *Exigent*. The name of the accused was then called out on five successive county court days. If the defendant had not come forward after that he was automatically outlawed by a decree of *Quinquies exactus*.

Thomas Uniacke was pronounced *Quinquies exactus*. He ignored the writs, as, like many of his fellow Catholics, he did not believe he could get justice in the Protestant courts and thought the process was a charade. He would not give the judicial system any credibility by taking part in it. Whether his limbs were to be chopped off and his entrails gutted and thrown on the fire, or whether his lands were to be forfeited, would not be decided by a mockery of a trial.

Politically, the Williamite victory marked the beginning of the Ascendancy, as the halcyon days of Protestant power in Ireland were later described. It led to the imposition of harsh penal laws. The Protestant minority felt insecure, and wanted to create a legal and economic buttress against further rebellion. The penal laws ensured that Catholics were excluded from having any political power. Concessions allowed by the Treaty of Limerick or royal prerogative were reversed or eroded by legislation.

In summer 1692, King William appointed a new lord lieutenant, Viscount Sydney, later earl of Romney. He arrived in Dublin at the end of August. By one of those most unpredictable flukes he was the man who would throw a lifeline to Thomas Uniacke, a person he had never met, and had even less interest in. Sydney set about preparing the legislative material for the new Irish parliament that was to sit in the autumn. But he was a man more renowned for pursuits of the flesh. And though he was over 50 years of age, young bosoms bursting through bodices more readily got his attention.

Sydney had been groom of the bedchamber to James, duke of York (later King James II), and master of the horse to the duchess of York when in his early twenties. He was considered to be 'extraordinarily handsome', and even earned the reputation of being 'the handsomest man of his time'. There were rumours that he had a dalliance with the duchess, and that the dedicated womaniser had vied with his friend, Henry Savile, for her attention. This resulted in a 'serious estrangement' between the duke and his wife. Whatever the truth of the stories, Sydney was dismissed with a great whiff of scandal.

His reputation was to follow him through life. It was rumoured he had 'a long standing intrigue with the wife of his nephew, Sunderland'. There was public scandal when he refused to provide for a former mistress and his illegitimate son. Grace Worthley was a widow and 'lady of good family', who had lived with Sydney for 20 years. He ignored her pathetic pleas for maintenance: 'I wish some good angel would instruct my pen to express something that would incline your lordship to moderate your hate towards me'. Reference to her health did not seem to soften his attitude when she complained: '... though I am perfectly lame and have in a manner quite lost the use of my limbs, yet my pen will never lose its vigour, nor will my tongue be silent'. While her creditors got more impatient, her tone to Sydney became more pleading: 'I wish you would consider that you must one day come to die, and that it will be too late when you come to lie upon your deathbed to wish you had been more kind and considerate of my sufferings.'

Sydney felt plagued by the woman. Being posted to Dublin must have been a welcome relief for him. But his reception from the Irish parliament was far from relaxing. The parliament Sydney presided over was a stormy affair. The Protestant parliamentarians had accused William of being too soft on popery, an accusation they also levelled at the viscount. Members alleged he was guilty of corruption and sympathetic towards papists and dissenters.

He weathered the attacks, and devoted most of his attention to the banquets and balls held in Dublin Castle for the ruling class of the metropolis and its environs. As lord lieutenant, Sydney made the most of a rather uninviting castle. He knew that it symbolised English rule in Ireland – and his authority. The venue could not compare with that of London, but was still full of beautiful young women to flirt with. He took pleasure in dancing with all the young women on these occasions, as well as the attractive married ones. He was a charmer, and his acumen in sexual diplomacy showed his political skills seriously wanting.

Margaret Uniacke, the second child of James Uniacke and Mary Neale, was only fifteen when her father died. In the summer of 1682, he had left Dublin with his wife for a place called Tunbridge Wells in England. He gave his daughter one final hug before he mounted the carriage parked outside their front door, the family's fashionable address in Back Lane. She knew her father was in bad health, but she probably never contemplated that he would never return. The family watched the carriage disappear down the road, rattling over the cobblestones, through the narrow streets of the capital to the port of Ringsend.

A letter arrived for their governess in late August, from their mother: their father was dead and buried in a small cemetery in the spa town where he had sought a restoration of his health.

Margaret had never said 'goodbye' to her father in the proper sense: seen him laid out at home and given a proper funeral. That might have helped her make sense of what had happened, to grieve and move on. Her mother came home without a husband, and had a family to support. It took her mother some years to regain any equilibrium in her life, and to some degree the happy rhythm of family life had been permanently disrupted.

When things were becoming normal again political crisis had descended upon the country. Margaret neither knew nor cared much about politics. The family did not revile Catholics – they had many Catholic relatives. But a claustrophobic fear had settled on the city as the repression of Protestants escalated. This was a traumatic experience for Margaret Uniacke. She was a young woman, ready to move out into society, to get married and have a family. The social status that the Protestant elite had enjoyed was gone. She had no prospect of going to banquets and meeting eligible young men, or having a suitable marriage arranged. Living in a state of constant fear, where there was little or no protection against being raped or murdered, took its toll.

It was an experience that inevitably must have hardened her, enamelling her to survive in a tough world, without the protection of a father. When her brother James was in danger of being arrested and fled Dublin to join the Inniskillingers, Margaret had to take on much of the responsibilities of the household. Many of her siblings were still children, while the elder ones had no prospects, and had been left nothing in their father's will.

The Battle of the Boyne had brought liberation to the Protestants of Dublin. But James Uniacke was still fighting most of the following year. There was little correspondence, and neither Margaret nor her mother knew if he were alive or dead. In April 1691 Mary Uniacke died. Her daughter was left to make the arrangements. After a sombre ceremony in the church of St Nicholas the following Saturday night, the coffin was carried gingerly through the black graveyard. Only the lantern carried by the sexton illuminated the gloom.

Later, with the younger siblings put to bed, Margaret sat at her father's old desk and opened the family Bible. In the lambent glow of candlelight, she wrote:

> *My dear Mother died the 30th day of April 1691, at five in ye morning, & was buried in St Nicholas' church on Saturday night following within ye walls of Dublin.*

By autumn, the war was over, and Margaret could rest assured that her brother was at least safe and well. Presumably, he visited the metropolis whenever he could, and found the social life in Dublin a welcome change from the drudgery of peacetime soldiering. The army career seemed the only future open to him. He did not choose to follow his father into the legal profession. James had inherited a huge fortune, a huge assistance to an impecunious young officer. It meant he was invited to all the social occasions in Dublin Castle, to which he brought his older sister Margaret, feeling strongly responsible for finding her a partner in marriage. She was now in her mid twenties. But there were also two other belles to introduce to society: Mary, 19 and Anne, 17. With his wealth, dowries were not a problem. But after the upheaval of the previous decade, good marriages could be difficult to arrange. The only other sibling was Norman, who was 13, and under the strict tutorage of a governor was completing his education, before embarking on a profession.

From the exterior, Dublin Castle looked a sinister place to the young Uniacke women. The carriage rattled noisily over the wooden planks of the drawbridge that crossed the dry moat. They entered the narrow arch guarded by a tower on either side. The prongs of the portcullis over their heads were like the teeth of a great monster, its mouth open wide to receive them. Then they found themselves in a cobbled courtyard, dimly lit by lanterns. The light did little to dispel the gloom of the place: sturdy towers dominated each corner, and battlements cast shadows through the last of the evening light. At the west end of the huge fortified complex was the king's banquet hall, its great oak doors open wide, light and music flowing out.

In the seductive glow of the hall the viscount would have been quick to see the three Uniacke sisters, standing demurely, as yet unaccustomed to the glitter of high society. Later, while in conversation with their brother about the prospects of promotion for the young officer, he could skilfully raise the issue of an introduction. The young women chattered nervously, flattered by the attention of this indulgent father-like figure.

The gossip suggested his initial conversations with Margaret Uniacke had been fruitful when she was seen on his arm at various social functions. An ostentatious display of new jewellery would reinforce the rumours – pearl drop earrings and necklaces, satin gowns, revealing bodices decorated with rosettes, chemises and skirts of only the highest quality, expensive shoes with dainty ribbons. The trend in feminine cosmetic fashion was to powder the face and wear a cheek patch, a mark considered a sign of beauty. Whether Margaret saw the lord lieutenant as a prospective husband, no one was sure. He was twice her age and a dedicated philanderer. Through his vanity, he could have maintained the debonair look of a younger man, with the most exclusive braided coats, waistcoats and exquisitely puffed out neck cloths. It was doubtful if he had the slightest intention of marrying anyone. But then Margaret Uniacke's motives were also suspect since she encouraged and responded to Viscount Sydney's advances – there had to be some motive.

Sydney's enemies were accusing him of profiting from his high position and taking bribes from Catholics in return for reversing their forfeitures. Rumours abounded that his mistress – as Margaret was believed to be – was also profiting from this enterprise. And indeed, she was. But she had the interests of her family at heart, those suffering under the current regime, most notably her uncle, Thomas, now dispossessed and facing ruin, even execution. One of the first things she did was to get her lover to grant him a royal pardon. From then on, she realised how she could influence the highest office in the country, the man with direct connection to the king himself. But she had to move fast, the political situation was uncertain. Velvet purses bulging with gold coins would discreetly change hands. Margaret became the link between her lover and the Catholic gentry desperate to be pardoned and get their properties back. She created a distance between the appellant and the lord lieutenant. It was known she could persuade him. In October, Sir John Morris of Knockagh paid her £500 for a pardon, £200 of which she gave to Thomas Uniacke to get him back on his feet. While Harvey Morris, who had been a member of James' Parliament, handed over £100, John Kerdiff of Dublin handed over £200 as the price to be paid. A later commission of enquiry presented these cases as evidence against her.

As 1693 wore on it became plain to Margaret that her lover's days were numbered. He too was losing interest. Every bed was only a temporary stay for him. The viscount could return to his life of luxury in London, but Margaret needed a new strategy if she were not to end up a destitute unmarried woman, shunned by respectable society.

14

The Conformed

James Uniacke must have looked particularly smart in his uniform of the king's own royal regiment of Irish Hussars. The coat was scarlet, lined and turned up with yellow, with matched yellow waistcoat and breeches, and riding boots stretching above the knee. The hat was round with broad brim, turned up at the sides and back. He would have cut a dashing figure with the young women. James was appointed a cornet in the regular army in March 1693, a dragoons regiment for the most part stationed in Ireland. Four years later, he received a commission as lieutenant under Captain Robert Stuart.

It appears that James Uniacke's regiment was stationed in Ireland throughout the 1690s. After the Peace of Ryswick, when William of Orange ended his war with Louis XIV of France, there was no need for such a large standing army. Consequently, Lieut Uniacke was among those reduced to half pay. By now, he was becoming restless: his army career was going nowhere, yet he had considerable wealth. He needed to make a decision about his life. Around 1700 he came to a decision. He would buy land in Cork, in the home of his ancestors, and become one of the country gentry. He did not sell up the Dublin house in Back Lane, but gave it over to his three sisters. His brother, Norman, was studying medicine in Trinity and had a promising future ahead of him.

In 1703, James Uniacke entered into negotiations with James Fitzgerald of Glenane to purchase the estate of Coolegorragh, just east of Youghal. Now Captain James Uniacke, he decided to build a home on his new estate befitting a man of his status. The house, situated on a height looking across a rich shapely countryside of pasture, meadow and copse, came to be known as Mount Uniacke. In 1706, he married Mary Matthews of Templelyon in Co. Wicklow, south of Dublin. Cork became home to the new family.

James' uncle, Thomas, was also rebuilding his life. His royal pardon and donation of money from his niece had given him a new sense of importance. His estates had escaped forfeiture, and he had escaped possible execution. These events emboldened him. Not long after the pardon, Thomas became involved in a violent and protracted dispute with the mayor and corporation of Youghal – a brave or foolhardy action for a Catholic in penal times. The two parties were in dispute over ownership of a town-land called Glengaddy. The corporation demanded he produce documents to prove his claim to the land. The issue became quite heated and the mayor ordered his men to forcibly occupy the land. He told them to 'break a gap, enter and claim said lands as the property of the corporation'.

The dispute was never to be settled in Thomas Uniacke's lifetime. But he had other dreams to follow. In the first years of the eighteenth century, he hired an architect to design a new house in the centre of Youghal, to reflect opulence and the latest in fashion. The man he commissioned was a Dutch architect called Leuventhen. The building was to be a sight of elegance and taste. A style of architecture known as Dutch Billy had be-come very fashionable. The influence is believed to have come to Ireland with the influx of linen and weavers from Holland, Flanders and France. The house was constructed of red brick, said to have been imported directly from the continent, at some considerable cost. Consequently, it became known as the Red House. Ironically, the design was a phenomenon of a growing Protestant contribution to Irish culture.

While the house rose brick by brick from its foundations so did the laws that would restrict the liberties and property rights of Catholics. Over the coming years through the efforts of what became known as the Penal Laws, their position became increasingly undermined. They were forbidden to bear arms or own a horse valued over £5. The popery bills limited the rights of Catholics concerning inheritance and leases. Catholic freeholders lost the right to vote.

While Thomas Uniacke had always been a fiery individual, old age made him increasingly cantankerous. The world he had known and loved all his life was gone. But if he could at least keep Roman Catholicism strong within his own family, he would at least contribute to its long-term survival and propagation. Yet, that too was becoming increasingly unachievable. His heir, Thomas, had a strong leaning towards the Protestant faith, his beliefs shaped by the Establishment on his mother's side of the family. To him his father's arguments were popery, idolatry and primitive. And it caused a bitter rift between the two men.

The dispute eventually led to litigation by the son against his father. In 1707 he took his case to the High Chancellor of Ireland alleging his father was denying him his entitlement as heir, while in contrast he had provided amply for his younger son, James. Thomas the elder had given the younger son a sizeable sum of money on his marriage to Austace FitzJames Ronayne in 1703. The eldest son insinuated his father was being petty and vindictive, while being in contrast 'so kind and indulgent to the said James and his wife, they both being papists'. On coming of age, Thomas insisted that he could not conform to the Roman Catholic faith. And on 27 August 1704, he publicly and openly embraced the Protestant belief in the parish church of Cloyne, east Cork. In his own words, he 'received the blessed Sacred of the Lord's Supper, according to the rights and ceremonies of the Church of Ireland'.

He charged that his father tried all methods to change the course of his conscience. He threatened that he would have to sell off large tracts of the estate if the son did not act as joint guarantor for a loan. The son refused, and alleged his father was trying to blackmail him into the clutches of popery, and effectively disinherit him and make him liable for any debts his father had accrued. At other times he showed a 'fatherly regard and kindness' towards his son. But when he finally realised he would not persuade Thomas junior to return to 'the Communion of the Romish Church' he cut him off from any financial assistance. If it were not for Protestant relatives, he 'might have perished for want of bread.' Thomas senior attempted to disinherit his son in his seething rage. But the law was on the son's side, as he well pointed out:

> ... By an act made in this kingdom in the second year of her present Majesty Queen Anne, entitled an Act for Prevention of further Growth of Popery; it is amongst other things enacted that from and after the 24th March 1703, upon complaint made in the honourable court by bill founded on the said Act, it shall be lawful for this honourable court to make such order for maintenance of every such Protestant child, not maintained by such popish parent, suitable to the degree and ability of such parent and to the age of such child ...

Because of his father's actions, he was now totally 'destitute of any subsistence or maintenance'. The twenty-seven year old wanted the court to grant an order of maintenance and discharge any liability for debts accrued by the father. That the debts 'should not remain as a clog upon the said estate when it shall please God that the same shall descend and come to your Orator as eldest son and heir of the said Thomas Uniacke, his father ...'

The elder Thomas Uniacke was a sad and bitter man. His son won his case – to his father he was no better than Judas. Now an old man in his sixties he did not have long to live. He had grown up in a time when his own Catholic beliefs had a place in the community, which united a family as brethren. As a young man, given a sound education by the monks, he had held out great hope in the forces of the Counter Reformation and the honour of the Stuarts. But the Cromwellian war, and its aftermath, was the darkest hour for the faith. He had not wavered in his resolve – but his own brother had. One of his nephews fought for William, and gloried in the Jacobite defeat. His own niece had prostituted herself for gain, and he had degraded himself by accepting her charity, in her influential role as vice-regal mistress. There was no way to reverse the course of history now. The Old English Catholic gentry were dead. On 8 April 1708 Thomas Uniacke, gentleman esquire, joined them, and was buried in St Mary's collegiate church, Youghal. He died, body and spirit broken. Cromwell had taken his final revenge.

Epilogue

For another two centuries, the Uniackes enjoyed the privilege of Ascendancy. In 1707, young Thomas married Helena Bor, the daughter of a Williamite general, Christian Bor, who had received lands in Co. Wexford as reward for his military service. The new Mrs Uniacke claimed to inject blue blood into the family's veins, 'that she was descended from a natural son of Henry IV of France, born before his accession'. The veracity of the story is unknown, but the tradition would have enhanced the Uniackes in elite social circles of Cork's Protestant gentry. And through marriage to the Purdon family of Co. Cork, later Uniacke genealogists could claim tenuous royal lineage to the Plantagenets, who ruled England in the thirteenth and fourteenth centuries. The Purdons had apparently traced their tree back to Princess Elizabeth, daughter of King Edward I.

Thomas Uniacke completed the Red House and it became his town residence. The family also bought the Woodhouse estate in Co. Waterford, near the village of Stradbally. Thomas erected a Georgian mansion near a quiet cove by the banks of the river Tay. Woodhouse became one of the notable demesnes along the south coast: over the years the family planted more than 150,000 ash and oak trees.

The house and its environs was visited by eighteenth- and nineteenth-century travellers. In *Egan's Waterford Guide*, published in 1894, the author, P. M. Egan, comments:

> *The demesne of Woodhouse is well worth the visit, scenes of dense wood and shingly dell opening at intervals into pretty lawns, which are watered by the river Tay. The river now and again bounds the pathway, as it escapes along rocky prominences, or under scrubby coverts making music for the traveller ... Woodhouse should prove*

Youghal enjoyed considerable prosperity during the eighteenth century. Her merchants traded with the European cities of Bristol, Bordeaux, Lisbon and Amsterdam as well as North America. The population grew rapidly, spreading out beyond the old medieval walls. The late eighteenth century saw the building of the Clock Gate in the centre of the town and the Mall House by the newly created tree-lined promenade on the water front.

The town's trade links gave it a cosmopolitan air. The colourful Bor Uniacke, eldest son of Thomas and Helena, became partial to soaking up the atmosphere. He chose to live in the Red House, apparently to escape the tranquillity of country life. He would sit with his Irish wolfhounds on the steps of his home in North Main Street, drinking claret. Bor would often invite the passer-by to join him in the celebration of Bacchus.

The other main branch of the family lived at Mount Uniacke. Captain James Uniacke, a professional soldier with no background in farming, made a very successful business of the estates purchased with his inheritance. He had spent a total of £3,230 sterling on his new endeavour.

One of Captain Uniacke's grandsons, also James, became a member of the Dublin parliament. He married Caroline Coote, daughter of Charles Coote of Coote Hill, and sister of the earl of Bellamont. In the early days of their marriage Lady Caroline, as she was commonly known, lived an extravagant and ostentatious lifestyle. Her coach, pulled by four horses, was a frequent sight on the roads round the estate. The coachmen aloft the carriage, in their white and scarlet Uniacke liveries, were quite a contrast to the ragged peasants working the fields, glancing up as the 'Lady' of the Mount passed by the hedgerows. But Caroline Uniacke's lifestyle changed after the birth of their only daughter, Prudence, as the child died in infancy and she became a virtual recluse. A sitting-room in the house became known as 'Caroline's room'. In the last years of her life, she never ventured beyond its four walls. She died in 1792, after 32 years of marriage.

During much of this period, James had been living a double life. He had been having an affair with a Catholic woman called Mary Higgins, who appears to have been a servant in the house. He had 10 children by this woman. When Caroline died, James Uniacke married his mistress and they had four legitimate children, who were brought up as Protestants. It appears that all 14 children lived as a family at Mount Uniacke. In his will James Uniacke, determined to look after all his offspring, left substantial sums of money to his illegitimate line to set them up for life. The legal recognition of this domestic arrangement – which would have caused scandal to family and society – had serious financial repercussions for the Mount Uniacke branch. The estate went into decline after James Uniacke's death in 1803.

The Uniacke family made a dramatic impact on the New World. In 1777, an ambitious lawyer, Richard John Uniacke, left Ireland for Canada. He settled in Nova Scotia, and later became its first attorney general. He acquired lands near Halifax, and built a splendid neo-classical mansion overlooking lakes and woodlands. The estate covered 4,200 acres and a small village, named Mount Uniacke, sprang up near the house. Richard John had 12 children by two marriages. One of his sons became prime minister of the province.

In the early nineteenth century, a John James Uniacke played a role in the exploration of the Antipodes. After an undistinguished time as a student at Cambridge University, he decided to sail for Australia in 1823, presumably to seek his fortune. There he met up with the explorer, John Oxley, and joined the expedition that discovered the Brisbane river. The stories he recorded of three escaped convicts they found, who had been living wild with the Aborigines, secured his place in Australian national biography. John James Uniacke was the second son of Robert of Woodhouse, an astute politician but poor manager of money. The young explorer did not live long. The harsh conditions of the new colony got the better of him and he died of an unspecified illness within 18 months. Twenty years later Robert Fitzgerald Uniacke, a grandchild of James Uniacke and Mary Higgins, followed in the footsteps of his cousin. There he married a Mary Anne Dunn, a Catholic.

As part of the ruling elite the Uniackes fought in Britain's wars. Robert John Uniacke of Woodhouse was an officer in the Seventh Hussars, serving in the Peninsular Wars and alongside Wellington at the Battle of Waterloo. Major James Uniacke of the Royal Marines was killed at the storming of Chin-Keang-foo, China, in 1842 during the Opium War. As a young Hussar officer, Charles Hill Uniacke saw action in the Crimea during the siege and fall of Sebastopol, and later campaigns in India. Captain James Uniacke, also of the Hussars, received the medal and order of the Iron Cross for his service during the Franco-Prussian war, in the early 1870s. Lieut Colonel James Crofton Uniacke was decorated for his part in the Sudan expedition of 1885. His son, Sir Herbert Crofton Campbell Uniacke, rose to the rank of general. He commanded the 5th Brigade, Royal Horse Artillery, of the British Expeditionary Force to France in 1914.

In the nineteenth century, many Uniackes are believed to have emigrated to America. It is most likely that this line was the Catholic progeny of James Uniacke and Mary Higgins, crossing the Atlantic in search of a better life. They made their contribution to the development of that great country. One of them played a role in a decisive episode of American history: Michael Uniacke of the Sixteenth New York Cavalry was involved in the capture of John Wilkes Booth, the assassin of Abraham Lincoln, at Garrett's Farm in 1865.

The Uniackes left their record through their soldiers, adventurers, lawyers and landlords – their legacy to both the world and the ascendancy.

Appendix I

Turbulence and Change 1536–1708

The purpose of this appendix is to give a historic summary of the period and to place events in context. It covers the years that the book deals with, but also the relevant preceding period.

By the mid sixteenth century, English involvement in Ireland had dated back some 400 years, to the arrival of Strongbow in 1169. Over the next four centuries, the English crown struggled to defeat the Irish and keep wayward Anglo-Irish lords in line. The focus of this essay is on the mid 1500s to early eighteenth century, and on that group of colonisers called 'The Old English', who were loyal to the king but still wished to retain and practise their Catholic beliefs.

When King Henry VIII broke with Rome, he put himself at the head of the Church; in matters of religion, his subjects were answerable to him, not to the pope. And in 1536, two years after the split, the Irish parliament made Henry 'Supreme Head on Earth of the whole Church of Ireland'. From this many consequences would flow. The king set about dissolving the monasteries. The effect of the Reformation was apparent only in the towns and the Pale – the hinterland of Dublin – and it had little impact on areas under Gaelic rule. In fact, the Reformation made little inroad into the Irish psyche. There was no popular resentment of the Catholic Church, as there was in England.

The Tudors tried to make the Irish and Old English conform. Queen Elizabeth I, Henry's daughter, met with fierce resistance to her efforts. Legislation only highlighted the religious divisions in Irish society: English Protestants on one hand, Old English and Gaelic Catholics on the other.

Elizabeth's greatest threat to her aim of subduing Ireland

came from Ulster. In 1559, Shane O'Neill – or Shane the Proud – succeeded his father as head of the O'Neill clan. Shane's father had renounced his claim to be an Irish king after he was given the title of Earl of Tyrone, and was content to live as a peaceful subject of the crown. In 1562, Shane travelled to London to meet the queen. Elizabeth wanted a compromise. Financial considerations were persuading her to seek a negotiated solution to her problems in Ireland. Shane was sent home with honour, and for the next five years ruled like a king. He would eventually be killed by his Ulster rivals, the O'Donnells.

While the settlement with Shane O'Neill had been a setback for Elizabeth's policy of surrender and re-grant, introduced by her father – whereby Gaelic chiefs would submit to English rule and be allowed keep their lands – the Elizabethans were making progress in other parts of the country. By the mid 1580s, the English largely controlled the provinces of Leinster, Munster and Connaught. Munster had been particularly difficult to bring to heel and in 1579, the Fitzgeralds of Desmond – Gaelicised Old English Catholics enjoying a high degree of independence over their territories – rebelled against the crown. The rising, led by James FitzMaurice Fitzgerald, cousin of the Earl of Desmond, was crushed with great severity. With the Desmond palatinate destroyed, the way was open for land confiscation and colonisation with Protestant English.

The clans of Ulster watched with unease as the rest of the island was increasingly colonised by new English settlers and old rulers were crushed. They knew that the authorities had designs on their lands as well. They saw no alternative but to resist. In 1595 Hugh O'Neill, Earl of Tyrone, joined with the other Ulster warlords to fight the English, and turn back the tide of Tudor colonisation. O'Neill was a brilliant military leader as well as a shrewd politician. The English viewed him as a serious threat as they believed he wanted to bring Ireland under Gaelic rule, with the aid of the pope and king of Spain.

For his part, O'Neill knew the English would never allow him establish palatinate jurisdiction over his territories. He also realised the need to extend the fight to the entire island and to enlist the support of Catholic Spain. O'Neill's army used highly successful guerrilla tactics against the English forces. Most of the engagements were skirmishes, but some of them turned into full battles, such as Clontibret in 1595. Two years later O'Neill was to win a major battle at the Yellow Ford. In 1601, a Spanish force landed at Kinsale on the south coast of Ireland. O'Neill and that other Ulster war lord, O'Donnell, set off to meet them – for a battle that would determine the fate of Gaelic Ireland.

The Battle of Kinsale was a decisive turning point in Irish history. The English, led by Lord Deputy Mountjoy, besieged the walled town, only to be surrounded by the Irish. But the Irish had little experience in the formal method of warfare that would follow and were quickly defeated. The Spanish surrendered the town and sailed home. This heralded the end of the Nine Years' War and the collapse of the Gaelic dynasties.

By the terms of the Treaty of Mellifont in 1603 – concluded just days after the death of Elizabeth I – both O'Neill and O'Donnell were allowed to keep their lands and live among their people in Ulster. But the situation had changed fundamentally: the English authorities now ruled every part of Ireland. In 1607, the two Ulster leaders set sail for the continent, in what came to be called 'The Flight of the Earls'. The leaders were resentful at having to be subjects of the English crown. But the move left their people defenceless and the English unhindered in their objective of colonisation – the plantation of Ulster had begun. This was an ambitious project, and ultimately far more successful than the Munster Plantation had been in the 1580s.

There were still many contacts between the Irish and the continent, particularly Rome. For this was the age of the Counter Reformation, the Catholic Church's fight back against the gains of Protestantism.

While England's authorities in Ireland had conclusively crushed Gaelic Catholicism, they had not defeated the Old English. By this time, the group had lost much of its political power. Yet they still owned one-third of the country's land, and were loyal to the crown – and English rule in Ireland. Much of their time was spent trying to persuade parliament of their loyalty to the English interest, and to forestall land forfeitures. But the Old English still had their uses.

When Charles I came to the throne in 1625, he immediately went to war against Spain. To finance the war he needed to borrow large sums of money. He promised the Old English sweeping concessions if they would lend him large sums of money. In the Graces, granted in 1628, Charles promised them the religious freedoms they were seeking. When the war ended, the king went back on his promise, leaving a taste of bitter mistrust.

In 1633, the king appointed Thomas Wentworth, the first Earl of Strafford, as Lord Deputy of Ireland. His ruthless ability made enemies of everybody. He built a strong and efficient administration, extracting money from the landed gentry – be they Protestant or Old English. He further weakened the power of the Old English by reducing their influence in the Dublin parliament, and making it harder for them to gain concessions from the king. He pushed through new land confiscations. And he penalised Protestant settlers in Ulster for not fulfilling the conditions of the land grants. When Wentworth was recalled to England in 1640, his enemies seized the opportunity to plot against him. To their great delight, he was executed for treason the following year.

King Charles was in growing dispute with the English parliament, which would soon erupt into civil war. The Old English used the opportunity to persuade the king to grant once again the Graces, though experience showed that promises were not enough. The Old English needed to have a greater control of the Dublin parliament. But Charles, who had already relinquished much of his power to the English parliament, would not concede any authority to the Irish parliament. The Old English had to settle for promises. Some Catholic landowners in Ulster became convinced that only force would win their demands. There was also a deep resentment at English rule and the sweeping plantation of the northern province. They wanted to recover their property and the status they had once enjoyed.

A plot was hatched to capture Dublin Castle, to coincide with a rising in Ulster. Things did not go exactly to plan: on 22 October 1641, the eve of the rebellion, the plotters in Dublin were arrested, after a drunken indiscretion had revealed details of the rising. The seat of government was secure, a serious blow to the rebels. The local rising in Ulster went ahead as arranged, led by Sir Phelim O'Neill. He denied he was rebelling against the king, but rather against the English parliament. In an effort to win support, O'Neill forged instructions from Charles, ordering Ulstermen to join the rebellion. And every follower had to take an oath of loyalty to the king.

The rebellion spread rapidly throughout Ulster. Protestant settlers were attacked; many were murdered or driven from their homes. The rebels then marched south to Dublin and had their first engagement with government troops just north of Drogheda in County Louth. Victorious, the Irish then besieged Drogheda itself. Many Old English in the area made common cause with the rebels. After all, they were loyal to the king and fighting against a Protestant parliament. The combined force became known as the Catholic Army.

During the early months of 1642, the war spread throughout Ireland. The rebels were enjoying some success until reinforcements began to arrive from England. By April, the Irish were being pushed back. Moreover, the English parliament was not willing to negotiate a peace – this was the opportunity to fully subdue Ireland. The English government was already raising money through the Adventurers Act, secured on the promise of confiscated land once the war was over.

In October 1642, the Irish met in Kilkenny and formed their own parliament to organise and direct the war efforts. The situation in England had radically changed at this stage: the king and parliament had gone to war. The civil war gave the Confederate Catholics, as they now called themselves, some leeway. The situation was becoming extremely confused. The king still maintained an army in Ireland under the command of the Earl of Ormonde. His main concern was to make peace with the Irish so he could concentrate on his fight with parliament. While parliament had substantial forces in Ireland, its first priority was – like Charles' – to win the English civil war.

The confederacy formed in Kilkenny had the motto – 'Ireland united for God, King and Country', but there were deep divisions. The Old English were amenable to agreeing moderate terms with Charles – they had the most to lose. The Gaelic Catholics, many of whom had returned from exile to fight, were extreme in their demands. They insisted on full recognition of Catholicism and the return of all lands confiscated from the Irish, and were opposed to any truce with the royalists. The Irish were more strident in the cause of the Counter Reformation, a position forcefully urged by Italian papal nuncio to the confederacy, Archbishop John Baptist Rinuccini.

The war dragged on throughout the 1640s, mostly uneventfully. The most outstanding Irish soldier was Owen Roe O'Neill, a nephew of Hugh O'Neill. He had spent years in the Spanish army and was convinced that English Protestant rule in Ireland had to be crushed. He defeated the English at the Battle of Benburb, County Tyrone, in 1646.

Both politically and militarily, the decade was wasted. A lot of time was spent haggling with the king, who eventually was defeated and beheaded in January 1649. Meanwhile the parliamentary forces were building in strength. And with the victory of the English civil war behind them, they could turn their attention to Ireland. They wanted to avenge the massacres of the 1641 rising, accounts of which had become greatly embellished through propaganda. It was a matter of defeating the brutish Irish and eradicating popery.

Oliver Cromwell, who came to prominence during the civil war as a brilliant cavalry commander, was appointed Lord Lieutenant of Ireland. In August 1649, he arrived in Dublin with his Puritan army, to finally subdue the Irish and mop up the last remnants of the royalist army led by James Butler, the first duke of Ormonde. Cromwell made speedy progress. In September, he besieged and captured Drogheda, and then marched on Wexford, which also fell with considerable ease. Many of Ormonde's garrisons capitulated without a fight. By the end of the year, Cromwell controlled the south and east of the country. Cromwell was recalled to London the following spring, but the war would continue until 1652.

Not many were executed after the war, the defeated soldiers were treated leniently enough: 30,000 of them were allowed to leave the country to fight in continental armies. Most of the deaths during the period 1649–1652 were probably due to social disruption and famine, as well as the devastating outbreak of bubonic plague in 1650.

The victorious began to implement the Cromwellian land settlement, though Cromwell had very little involvement in carrying out the programme itself. This became the job of the English parliament and the policy-makers did have trouble in persuading Protestants to move over to Ireland. As a result, the Irish tenants and labourers were allowed to remain on the land. The real target for the puritans were the landowners, who fell into two categories: those who had been involved in the 1641 rebellion and those who had not. The first were to forfeit their estates and property rights. The second were to transplant to another part of the country and receive a reduced amount of land, usually of inferior quality.

For this ambitious social engineering plan to work, a comprehensive survey of all the land in Ireland had to be undertaken – a massive task. Sir William Petty, a scientist and statistician, directed the main survey. He was considered one of the most gifted men of his generation.

Those to be transplanted were to move to Connaught or County Clare, west of the river Shannon. The remaining parts of the country still in Irish or Old English hands became the property of the government and were used to pay the government's creditors, the adventurers who had financially and materially supported the war. Land was also granted to officers and soldiers in lieu of pay. Many sold out to larger grantees. In fact, many of the gentry who forfeited their lands stayed where they were, and managed the estates, albeit as tenants, for the new landowners.

In 1660, two years after the death of Cromwell, the Stuart monarchy was restored. Catholic royalists were hopeful of some sympathy from the king, whose father they had most loyally supported. In return, they felt they had a right to expect religious toleration and the return of their lands. Indeed, Charles II was sympathetic to their grievances, but, as always, the politics were complicated. The new king had been recalled by the commonwealth parliament, which insisted the land settlement remain untouched. Charles made promises to both sides.

Charles did attempt to resolve the problem. In 1662, he introduced the Act of Settlement, whereby innocent Catholics were to get their lands back and Cromwellian settlers were to be compensated with land of equal value – but such land could not be found. A court of claims was set up to adjudicate on petitions from Catholics. But there was strong Protestant hostility at a scheme they saw as being promiscuously lenient towards the Catholic gentry. The duke of Ormonde, who was now lord lieutenant, recommended to the king that the terms should be modified. The Act of Explanation followed to explain the first act. It stated that settlers should give up one-third of their lands to Catholics. Recovery was to prove a slow and arduous pursuit. Most claimants were left unsatisfied. Overall, Catholic landlords were better off under Charles, though they only regained a fraction of their original estates. At the beginning of the 1640s, they owned about two-thirds of the land: by the end of the restoration, they had only one-fifth.

The Catholic gentry enjoyed a reasonable degree of religious tolerance during the restoration period. Ormonde was practical in his approach: if they recognised the king, they could practise their religion quietly. The duke demanded Catholics sign a declaration, the Remonstrances, recognising the king's authority in all matters temporal. This was unacceptable to the Catholic Church and no agreement was reached. For most of the time there was peaceful coexistence though events sometimes turned ugly, for example the 'popish plot' in England and the trial and execution of Archbishop Oliver Plunkett, accused of treason and a Catholic conspiracy.

Commercially the 1660s and 1670s were prosperous years, a prosperity Catholic landowners also enjoyed. The meat, butter and wool trades flourished. This was despite trade restriction imposed by the English parliament on Irish trade. While Protestants held the overwhelming share of the land and wealth, there was still a vibrant Catholic nobility made up of landed gentry, merchants and lawyers. This group would account for a significant Old English revival in the 1680s.

In 1685, Charles II died and was succeeded by his brother, James II, a Catholic. In Ireland Catholics were filled with joy: Protestants with alarm, though the new king tried to assure the Protestant population they had nothing to fear. But the actions of the Earl of Tyrconnell, Richard Talbot, were far from convincing. The Catholic lord was determined to pursue the Catholic interest in Ireland. He was made viceroy in 1687 and began reorganising the army by dismissing Protestant officers and replacing them with Catholic ones. Catholic judges and privy councillors were appointed. More key posts in the Dublin administration were filled with Catholics. Preparations were made for a Catholic parliament, which convened in 1689. Many Protestants left for England. There were profound structural changes taking place to radically reverse the land confiscations of previous years.

But Tyrconnell's plans were thwarted by events in England, where the rule of a Catholic was unpopular. In 1688 William of Orange, the son-in-law of James II, was invited by members of the Protestant establishment in England to overthrow the papist monarch. Unpopularity at home and an invasion by William from his home in the Netherlands forced King James to flee to France, and seek the protection of Louis XIV. William III and Mary II were enthroned as joint monarchs.

In March 1689, James landed in Ireland with French money and arms. Ireland was the only part of his realm still loyal to him, and a stepping-stone to the recovery of the throne. Later that year he called a parliament in Dublin. The sittings debated the fundamental issues. But decisions and their implementation were predicated on James defeating William of Orange in the approaching war – a war that was to be fought on Irish soil. It was to be a war between two kings, two religions. Ireland was merely the battlefield, a sideshow in a continental war. William was allied with the Holy Roman Emperor and the Catholic king of Spain against Catholic France. For the Irish the coming conflict was about local ownership of land, religious freedom and political power.

The Protestants of Ulster resisted James, and the three-month Jacobite siege of Derry began. In other parts of the north, the Inniskillingers, a force of dragoons that attracted young men from all round the country, had considerable success against James' forces. The actions in Ulster preserved a vital bridgehead for the Williamite army to land. William arrived in Ireland in June 1690. On 1 July, the two armies met at the river Boyne in Co. Meath.

The Williamite army was 36,000 strong, made up of English, Dutch, Danes, Germans and Huguenots. The ethnically diverse composition reflected the European context of the battle. The Jacobite army was 25,000 strong, mostly Irish but also 7,000 French. After some difficulty, William's troops managed to cross the tidal river. Once across, victory was theirs. The Irish put up a brave fight – especially its cavalry. But James made a critical error at the early stages of the battle: noting that a section of the enemy was moving downstream, he mistakenly thought the main attack was to take place farther west, so moved the bulk of his army to meet them. The Jacobites were in a loop on the river, so were at risk of being cut off. But the analysis was wrong: the main thrust was at the village of Oldbridge, where the two armies had been facing each other since the day before. James had split his smaller force. When the attack came, defeat was inevitable.

The vanquished James fled the battlefield back to Dublin. Within a few days, he left the country for permanent exile in France. While the Boyne was a serious blow for the Irish, the army remained largely intact. It regrouped outside Dublin then retreated west to Limerick on the river Shannon. The ensuing Williamite siege was unsuccessful. Furthermore, the Irish were heartened by the exploits of the heroic cavalry officer, Patrick Sarsfield. He sallied out and ambushed William's siege train en route from Dublin. William of Orange needed to return to the continent and the siege was lifted.

When the campaigning resumed in 1691 Sarsfield was in effective command of Limerick. A Dutch general called Ginkel was now leading the Williamite army. He attacked across the Shannon at Athlone. The decisive battle of the war took place at Aughrim, where the Irish were unequivocally beaten. Once again, they retreated to Limerick, pursued by the enemy. Once again, Limerick was besieged. But this time it was short-lived. Sarsfield believed it was pointless to go on and thought it best to negotiate a settlement. William was also anxious to end the war and move his troops to Flanders where the French were pressing him hard. Some hard bargaining followed and, on 3 October 1691, the Treaty of Limerick was signed.

Sarsfield left Ireland with 14,000 of his fellow countrymen. These soldiers would make a name for themselves on the battle-fields of Europe. Sarsfield was killed two years later at the Battle of Landen. There were generous terms for those who chose to stay: they were allowed right of worship and property. Irish Pro-testants thought the terms too generous and did everything they could to undermine and erode the terms of the treaty.

1691 ushered in the era of the Penal Laws and the Protes-tant ascendancy, a social elite where power and wealth were confined to that privileged minority. The Irish parliament – now completely Protestant – set about introducing laws to remove the economic and political power of Catholics, thereby increas-ing their own security. Frequently the Protestant community was at odds with King William, who they saw as being too lenient to Catholic grievances. They also accused Lord Lieutenant, Vis-count Sydney, of corruption in helping Catholic gentry get their forfeited lands back.

It would not be until the end of the eighteenth century that the severe laws against Catholicism would begin to be relaxed.

Chronology

1536: Henry VIII 'supreme head on earth' of the Church in Ireland; begins dissolving the monasteries.
1547: Death of Henry VIII.
1558: Accession of Elizabeth I.
1559: Shane O'Neill, or Shane the Proud, becomes head of the O'Neill sept.
1562: Shane O'Neill travels to England to meet Queen Elizabeth.

1569: Shane O'Neill killed by the O'Donnells.

1579: Beginning of the Desmond rebellion led by James FitzMaurice Fitzgerald.

1595: Hugh O'Neill, Earl of Tyrone, goes to war against the English.

1595: Hugh O'Neill wins battle of Clontibret.

1597: Hugh O'Neill wins the Battle of Yellow Ford.

1601: The Battle of Kinsale.

1603: The Treaty of Mellifont.

1603: Death of Queen Elizabeth, accession of James I of England.

1607: 'The Flight of the Earls'.

1625: Charles I comes to the throne of England.

1628: The Graces.

1633: Thomas Wentworth made Governor of Ireland.

1641: Start of the Irish rebellion.

1642: Confederacy formed in Kilkenny.

1642: Civil war breaks out in England between the king and parliament.

1646: English force defeated by the Irish at the Battle of Benburb.

1649: Charles I is beheaded after royalists are defeated by parliament.

1649: Oliver Cromwell arrives in Ireland, to avenge the massacre of Protestants in 1641 rebellion.

1649: Cromwellian forces take Drogheda and Wexford, make Youghal their winter quarters.

1650: Outbreak of bubonic plague.

1650: Cromwell recalled to England.

1652: Cromwellian war ends and land settlement begins.

1658: Oliver Cromwell dies.

1660: Charles II is crowned king.

1662: Ormonde created Lord Lieutenant.

1662: The Act of Settlement is introduced.

1663: The Court of Claims.

1665: The Act of Explanation.

1681: Execution of Archbishop Oliver Plunkett.

1685: Charles II dies; Catholic brother James II becomes king.

1687: Earl of Tyrconnell made viceroy, introduces
Pro-Catholic measures.

1688: James is overthrown, in favour of his son-in-law
William of Orange.

1689: James arrives in Ireland and calls an Irish parliament.

1689: The siege of Derry.

1690: Battle of the Boyne; William defeats James.

1690: The first siege of Limerick.

1691: The Battle of Aughrim.

1691: The second siege of Limerick.

1691: Sarsfield signs Treaty of Limerick and leaves for the
continent.

1691–1708: Many of the penal laws restricting the religious and
property rights of Catholics introduced.

Appendix II

A Historic Sketch of Youghal

The town of Youghal is situated on the estuary of the river Blackwater in County Cork on the south coast. The name comes from the Irish *Eochaill*, meaning 'yew wood', creating a picture of what the landscape looked like hundreds of years ago, when Ireland was covered in thick deciduous forests.

The area was inhabited from prehistoric times. But it was the seafaring Vikings who first made use of its natural attributes as a harbour. The Norse people were both traders and raiders, in time settling down to follow purely commercial activities. A settlement grew up along a strip of flat land on the eastern shore, at the foot of a steep embankment that levelled out onto plateau stretching west through fertile fields and forests. The Viking settlement was small but well fortified. There was often hostility between themselves and the Celtic Irish. In 864 AD, a powerful local tribe, the *Deisi*, destroyed the settlement.

Even at an early stage of its history, Youghal was an important commercial centre. It was linked by road (*Bealach Eochaille* in Irish) to the rich monastery community of Lismore in County Waterford – a place frequently attacked by the Vikings before they became more sedentary and converted to Christianity.

In the twelfth century, the Normans arrived from England. Landing in Wexford in 1169 they gradually spread throughout the island. Their military superiority assured them victory. The English king, Henry II, granted the area round Youghal to Robert Fitzstephen in 1177, who later passed the estates to his half brother, Maurice Fitzgerald, ancestor of the earls of Desmond.

The Normans brought a new social concept to Ireland – the town. They made good use of the natural characteristics of Youghal: they transformed it into a thriving walled town and major mercantile port. In the thirteenth century, it attracted settlers from Britain, and forged a strong link with the city of Bristol. By about 1350, Youghal was trading with ports in Britain, northwest Europe and the Mediterranean, importing wines, spices and salt while exporting wool, timber and fish. A beacon tower was constructed to guide vessels safely across the sandbar at the entrance to the harbour.

According to the *Annals of Youghal* dated 1353, '*the Freemen of Yoghill were allowed freedom in trade in the different staples throughout England and Wales, for wool, leather, woolfells and lead*'. Another entry in the annals shows the cosmopolitan nature of the town and the rivalry it caused. Some Flemish traders had been granted special privileges by the king to trade, but '*the Yoghel burghers jealously resisted these concessions; and William de Vesci, the Deputy, at their instance, laid detainers on the ships of the foreigners.*'

The walled defences of the town boasted at least twelve towers. The walls climbed from south and north ends of the docks up the steep slopes to the west wall on the higher ground overlooking the town. The narrow main street dissected the town between the South and the North gates, with narrow lanes like ribs leading to the harbour or upwards towards the top west wall and St Mary's church, founded in the thirteenth century, and enlarged over following centuries. A twice-weekly market was held in the main street, the focal point being the market cross. Nearby stood the market house, where officials did their business, and the tholsel, where the mayor and corporation met. The streets and lanes were narrow and dark, but during the day there was a constant bustle of life. The taverns were full of traders and sailors, with tales of strange lands and peoples – some of whom even came ashore at Youghal.

The town was laid out in burgage plots, strips of land behind the houses. The dwellings faced on to the street, with the plots – for growing vegetables and keeping domestic animals – stretched up to the higher ground. In 1300, Youghal had 240 burgages.

Two religious houses were built outside the walls: a Dominican friary to the south, which became known as South Abbey; and the Franciscan Friary just outside the North gate, called North Abbey. A small Benedictine house, St John's Priory, was established on Main Street. Thomas Fitzgerald, Seventh Earl of Desmond, founded the College of Youghal in 1464. The institution gained international recognition: Pope Innocent VIII referred to it as 'University of the City of Youghal'. It was constructed beside St Mary's, which became known as St Mary's Collegiate Church.

The fifteenth century saw other developments in Youghal. A walled extension called the Base Town was added to the south. A new quay was built alongside it, and accessed through the Watergate, which would become a busy thoroughfare for merchandise over the following three hundred years. The construction of a fortified townhouse symbolised prosperity brought by commerce, but also the need for security. Such buildings were used to store valuable goods as well as to accommodate families. Originally built for the Walsh family, it was later purchased by Sir Robert Tynte, who married the widow of poet Edmund Spenser. Author of *The Fairie Queene* Spenser lived at Kilcolman Castle near Doneraile in North County Cork.

The Earls of Desmond were powerful Anglo-Irish magnates in the province of Munster since the twelfth century. Their power was so great that they aroused the suspicion of the authorities in Dublin and that of the crown. When Henry VIII broke with Rome he dissolved the monasteries and began a programme of legislating against Catholicism. The Desmonds were Catholic and would not countenance any diminution of their political or religious rights.

The second half of the sixteenth century was a time of turmoil, with the Desmonds in conflict with Queen Elizabeth. The struggle entered its final chapter in 1579 when James Fitzmaurice, cousin of the Earl of Desmond, returned from the continent to start a rebellion. Soon the whole sept was drawn into the war.

Desmond attacked the English garrison in Youghal. The dilapidated walls of the town were unable to withstand the assault. The town was soon taken, and with some ferocity by all accounts. According to the *Council Book of Youghal*, the town 'was not habitable for some time afterwards'. The soldiers desecrated St Mary's Collegiate church, by that time a symbol of the Anglican faith and many of the Catholic townsfolk joined them in the destruction.

The English, led by the Earl of Ormonde, retook the town. One of his first acts was to execute the mayor, Patrick Coppinger, for failing to protect the town. Coppinger was hanged from the window of his own house in the main street. The rebellion was finally crushed in 1582. Desmond's lands were confiscated, and 40,000 acres – including Youghal – passed into the hands of Sir Walter Raleigh, the English adventurer. Raleigh became a major landowner in Munster after the defeat of the Desmond Rebellion. But he had little success in attracting settlers over from England – Ireland was still seen as a wild and dangerous place.

On his visits to Youghal Raleigh stayed at his residence, Myrtle Grove, beside St Mary's. He was mayor of the town in 1588 and 1589. In 1602, he sold his estates to Richard Boyle, an ambitious adventurer and entrepreneur, who would later become the first earl of Cork. Boyle was born in Canterbury and came over to Ireland in his early twenties. He had plenty of ambition but no money. Yet, Boyle was a man who made and seized opportunity. And he was more successful than Raleigh in settling the land he purchased.

Boyle was influential in getting a new charter for Youghal, which greatly enhanced the potential of the town. Exports from Youghal, at the beginning of the seventeenth century, included pipe staves, wool and cattle, while the booming town imported luxury items such as wines, cloth and tobacco. Boyle owned several residences in Ireland, including Lismore Castle and the old college in Youghal, which he converted into a sumptuous mansion. He also built the almshouse in the centre of the town, a statement of his benevolence and wealth.

Boyle was made earl in 1620 and played an important role in defending Youghal during the years of rebellion in the early 1640s. He died in 1643, while the country was still in conflict and turmoil. He was buried in the south transept of St Mary's, where he had constructed a tomb befitting a man of his status. The elaborate and ornate monument depicts the earl, with his first and second wife, and some of his fifteen children. It reminds both congregation and visitor that Boyle had been a significant benefactor of the church: he had financed extensive renovations, building a new roof and repairing the tombs of its founders.

The Earl of Cork helped garrison the town, a defence that paid off well. At one point, the rebels used cannon from across the estuary at Ferrypoint, pounding the tightly packed streets of Youghal. Ferrypoint was the only crossing point for travellers from the east and north of the river Blackwater, the last leg of the journey being made by boat from the low sandy spit of land stretching into Youghal Bay.

Despite the greatest efforts of the Irish to force the town to surrender, the English still managed to get reinforcements through, running the gauntlet of the rebel cannon. Admiral William Penn was rewarded with lands in Cork for his efforts to get supplies to the besieged garrison in 1645. His son, also William, was the founder of Pennsylvania in the United States.

The townsfolk of Youghal had much to preoccupy them during these years: the countryside was wasted, livestock and crops destroyed. Hunger and hardship were constant factors in everyday life. Probably little attention was given to the raging civil war in England between King Charles I and parliament.

With the victory of parliament, Charles was beheaded and England became a republic, under the name of the commonwealth. Determined to finally crush the Irish rebels and the last remnants of the royalist army, parliament dispatched a force led by Oliver Cromwell.

Fear gripped the town when news of Cromwell's approach reached its people. Tales spread of atrocities being committed against the Irish. The inhabitants lived under a threatening shadow when the Cromwellian forces made Youghal their winter quarters. Cromwell is said to have made the old Benedictine house in North Main Street his headquarters. Six months later, after his spring campaign, Cromwell left Youghal, riding at the head of a cavalcade of Roundheads, through the medieval Water Gate on the quays. The naval frigate, *President*, awaited him. He sailed from Ireland never to return. Afterwards the Water Gate became known locally as Cromwell's Arch, the last place in Ireland to hear the thundering hooves of his horse.

Youghal, like the rest of the country, was to suffer over the next ten years. Famine, plague and displacement ravaged the whole island. The Catholic gentry of Youghal faced transplantation and disinheritance. The trade once so important to the port was wiped out. But with the restoration of the Stuarts, prosperity once again returned. The 1660s and 1670s were decades of relative prosperity and religious tolerance. When Catholic James II succeeded his brother, Charles II, as king, things changed radically for Catholics in Ireland. The civil institutions of the state came under Catholic control. In 1689 Thomas Uniacke, esq., and Edward Gough were elected by Youghal Corporation to represent the borough in James' new Dublin parliament.

But things were to radically change. James was defeated at the Battle of the Boyne. The Catholic-dominated borough in Youghal collapsed and the town surrendered to William of Orange. 1691 saw the end of the war between the two kings, and the town of Youghal settled down into a new age of the elite

Protestant ascendancy. The town was to see huge changes in the eighteenth century. But ironically, one of the most prestigious examples of the new century was the Red House in North Main Street. Its construction was begun in the early 1700s by Catholic Thomas Uniacke, though finally completed by his Protestant son after the father's death.

Youghal saw considerable economic growth in the eighteenth century. The quays were expanded and new warehouses built. Sailing ships lined the docks, carrying on a vibrant trade with maritime cities such as Bristol, Liverpool, Bordeaux, Lisbon and Amsterdam. There was also a significant transatlantic trade. The town soon spread out beyond its medieval walls. The overseas trade and its ecumenical mix of Catholic, Anglican, Quaker, Huguenot, Presbyterian and Methodist gave Youghal a multicultural profile.

Perhaps Youghal's most famous architectural landmark, the Clock Gate, was built in 1777. It replaced Trinity Gate in Main Street. The distinctively appealing new gate was incongruously used as a prison until the mid-nineteenth century. During the 1798 rising, several Irish rebels were hanged from the windows of the tower.

The Mall House, now used as the town hall, was constructed in 1779. Youghal was developing an air of graceful elegance: a tree-lined promenade had been built along the seafront. Round this time, the town was becoming a fashionable holiday resort. In the nineteenth century, Youghal attracted swimmers and holidaymakers to White Strand, advertising the amenity as 'the one bright spot/ Miles of silver strand'.

The Victorian era was a time of mixed fortunes for Youghal. Traditional industries were affected by changing markets and punitive British legislation against Irish exports. While a lighthouse, operational to this day, was erected on the site of the medieval beacon tower, Youghal was becoming less attractive as a port. The development of larger ships made the sandbar at the harbour entrance a more serious obstacle to navigate. Shipping moved to places like Cork and Waterford, for the deep-water facilities. But other industries expanded during the nineteenth century: fishing, brickmaking and lace work. Tourism was further aided by the opening of the railway line from Cork in 1860, turning Youghal into an easily accessible seaside town.

Ferrypoint, which had shuttled travellers across the Blackwater since the middle ages finally became redundant: in 1832, a wooden bridge was constructed just north of the town. An iron bridge replaced it in the 1880s. The present bridge was erected in 1963.

Youghal was famous for its lace in the nineteenth century. The industry was set up by local nuns to provide employment after the Great Famine of 1845–1849. The driving force was a Sister Mary Ann Smith. She taught herself the stitches of a small piece of antique Italian lace, then went on to teach others the skill. In 1852, the convent opened a lace school. It was soon producing high quality lace.

In 1863, Princess Alexandra was presented with a shawl made from Youghal lace as a wedding present when she married the Prince of Wales, later King Edward VII. Over the years, the beautifully crafted lace work was presented to many dignitaries and royals. One of the finest pieces ever made contained over five million stitches. It was made in six months by 60 lace-makers working day and night and was created for Queen Mary to wear on her visit to India in 1911.

The product achieved great success, being presented at international exhibitions. But by the twentieth century, changes in fashion and technology reduced the market for handmade lace. Production of Youghal lace went into decline after the First World War.

Brick-making was another important industry for over 200 years from the eighteenth century. The local clay is also particularly suitable for pottery. The 1700s saw a sharp increase in the amount of brick and pottery work being made. Between 1808 and 1815, the brickworks in the town provided the material for barracks and Martello Towers in the region, and even for colonial fortifications as far away as Barbados. Products made in Youghal included household items and decorative ware as well as bricks.

The fortunes of Youghal continued to decline after Irish independence in 1922. But in the 1950s, new industries were establishing themselves in the town. The most famous was Youghal Carpets, opening in 1954 with just four employees. At its height, the company employed over 3,600 staff, 800 of them in the Youghal factory. The fine quality of its wool carpets brought it worldwide renown. The company also had operations in Britain and in continental Europe. But market conditions changed and Youghal Carpets was finally forced to close its factory doors in 1984.

Today, much of Youghal's manufacturing industry is gone. The waterfront, which had witnessed so much history and contributed so much prosperity, is now chiefly a recreational amenity for pleasure boating and sailing. Modern Youghal has a prosperous air, and much to impress the visitor. In addition to the marine activities, the town has retained much of its historic character. The layout of the main street and connecting streets has not changed much in 800 years. A short walk up Friar Street, through what was the base town, leads to the Clock Gate, now housing a genealogical centre. Past the attractive nineteenth century shop fronts is a concealed relic of medieval Youghal: a small wooden door and stone arch – the original entrance of St John's Priory. The Red House, a private residence, still stands on North Main Street, opposite a busy shopping centre.

Steep, narrow Church Street leads up to St Mary's, the Romanesque cruciform-shaped building still in use today as the Church of Ireland place of worship. In the grounds stands a feudal tower house, now used as the belfry. In the cemetery gravel paths zigzag upwards through rows of slanted lichen-covered headstones and tombs, overgrown, the iron railings rusting. From the top of the graveyard, steps ascend to the medieval walls, to a sweeping view of the town, the estuary and the countryside beyond.

Youghal has managed to retain much of its historic character, the gateway to the past.

Appendix III

The Last Will and Testament of Maurice Uniacke of Ballyvergin

I, *Maurice Uniacke of Youghal, in the County of Cork, Alderman, being, God be praised, in perfect health, sense and memory, do make this, my last will and testament, in manner and form following --*

I do bequeath my soul to God Almighty, my Maker and Redeemer, and ordain my body to be interred and buried in my ancestral burial or chapel in the South Abbey of Youghal, if licence thereof be had for love or money, otherwise in my father's chapel in Our Lady's Church in Youghal Aforesaid.

I do appoint and ordain my son and heir, Thomas Uniacke, to be executor of my last will and testament, and to see the contents thereof in all points to be accomplished and performed.

I do bequeath unto my son, James Uniacke, one stone house or messuage in Youghal aforesaid, wherein one John Griffin lately dwelled, and also the five enclosures or meadows of land, lying in the burgagery of Youghal aforesaid, now leased to Theobald Ronayne of the same, Alderman.

I do bequeath and leave unto my son, Edmond Uniacke, one messuage or stone house and garden in Youghal without the south gate, now in the tenure and occupation of William Murfye, Wollencomber, and formerly leased to Thomas Holdshipp; and one other stone house without the south gate of Youghal aforesaid, called by the name of the 'Sign of the Sun', with the stables, cottages and gardens there unto belonging; and four enclosures or meadows adjoining one to another, now in the possession of Nicholas Gallwan, on the south side of Cork Lane by the Spittle of Youghal.

I do bequeath and leave unto my daughter, Austace Uniacke, for her preferment in marriage, when she shall arrive at the age of sixteen years, the sum of two hundred pounds sterling, to be paid unto her by my son and heir out of my estate in inheritance and moveable goods.

I do bequeath and leave unto my daughter, Joane Uniacke, the sum of one hundred pounds sterling.

I do leave and bequeath all my estate of inheritance and moveable goods unto my wife, Margaret Uniacke, during the minority of my children, for and during her natural life for her own maintenance and theirs, and the good holding and occupation of them, and, if she marry that then she shall have the third part of all my estate and means.

I do leave and bequeath unto my son, Richard Uniacke, one messuage or stone house lying without the south gate of Youghal, lately in the tenure of Edward Stoute, Alderman, with a garden thereunto belonging, together with a hundred and forty pounds which the said Stoute standeth in arrears out of the said house; and one enclosure or lot of ground, lying near Parkrullany, or Dollinsparke, without the north gate of Youghal, lately in the possession of William Uppington; and also two enclosures or parks, called by the name of St John's Park without the south gate of Youghal.

I do bequeath unto my said son and heir, Thomas Uniacke, the two houses of my ancestors in Youghal Aforesaid, together with all such houses, lands, tenements, and hereditaments whatsoever in Youghal, Kinsale, and in the county of Cork, which I hold by estate of inheritance, or hereafter mentioned or bequeathed by this my last will and testament, together with all such reversions that may happen, which, with all other my lands, tenements, and hereditaments whatsoever, I do appoint and ordain my overseers to put to the best use on behalf of my said son and heir, towards the payments of my debts and legacies, and also the estate of the rest of my said children to their best use, profit and behalf, until they shall come to years of discretion.

I do leave unto my son, Thomas, Aforesaid, my signet, with a new damaske cloth and napkins, and a press cloath.

I do (in discharge of my conscience), by this my last will and testament bequeath and leave unto the Almes House in Youghal by the quay, the sum of twenty shillings sterling for ten years to come, to be paid every Easter day.

I do bequeath and leave forty shillings to be distributed among the poor native widows of this town of Youghal.

I do declare to the world that I intend to die with the habit of the Seraphical order of St Francis, which I desire may be wrapped on my body after my decease from this transitory world, and do hereby appoint my wife to bestow on the convent of that order at Youghal, when it shall be settled and established for that purpose, the sum of five pounds sterling. Also I desire my wife to bestow on the convent of the Order of St Dominic, so settled here as foresaid, the sum of forty shillings. Moreover, I do leave to Father Jasper Galwan the sum of thirty shillings, to be given him by my wife aforesaid, and he to remember to pray for my soul after my death every Sunday while he lives. And finally, I leave my blessing with my wife and children to be pleased and contented with what I left them by this my last Will and Testament.

In witness that this is my last Will and Testament, I have to the same put my hand and seal, the day and year above written.

An addition to the former will, 9 February 1648.

I do bequeath unto my son, John, one messuage or stone house, known by the name 'Custom House', and also one other house lately in the possession of David Downy, also the several enclosures of ground known by the name 'Moniremine, Monergarriff', and four enclosures of ground holden by Edward Gough in mortgage of forty pounds.

I do bequeath and leave unto my daughter, Joane Uniacke the sum of one hundred and three score pounds sterling.

I do bequeath and leave unto my sister, Christen Uniacke, the sum of five pounds sterling, and that to her to be paid in corn in the next year's crop as the market goes.

I do bequeath and leave unto my servant Nell Bluett the sum of five pounds sterling, to be paid in corn in the next year's crop.

I do by these presents nominate, constitute, and appoint my well beloved cousin, Richard Fitzgerald, Esquire, of Rostelane, my brother (in law) Nicholas Miagh, and my brother Edmond Uniacke, to be overseers of my wife and children, and this my last Will and Testament, and also to convert and dispose of all things herein expressed and declared to the best use and benefit of my said wife and children. Also I do appoint by my overseers to have a special care of my Writing and Evidence and concern my estate, which remain in one trunk by me left in the custodie of my cousin Robert Bluett, Esquire, now Sofferaigne of Killmallock, who left the same for more safety with one Nicholas Kearney of the same, gentleman, to be kept during these troubled times, and my will is that my said cousin and my overseers, shall lock with two keys a piece with them, until such time as they may remove the said trunk from thence unto my wife's custody when the times are settled, and if there be occasion to open the said trunk for the avail of my said children, and when my said son and heir before mentioned shall come to the age of twenty and one years, to deliver the said trunk and evidences into his own hands and possession. Till such time the said trunk is in the custody and keeping of Nicholas Gallwan.

Signed MAURICE UNIACKE.

Being present after signing and sealing hereof – Jasper Gallwan, Charles oge McCarthy (his mark), Nicholas Miagh, Patrick Forrest.

Sources

Cromwell's Revenge: A True Story was born of a three-year labour of love, for the Uniackes are not simply dusty names from the past, subjects of a detached academic exercise – they are my family, my genes. My paternal grandmother's maiden name was Uniacke, and for many years, their story had fascinated me, begging to be told.

My endeavours led me to primary sources that hitherto had not been investigated. But I am most deeply indebted to those who have undertaken the vast bulk of the scholarly research upon which I have based this book – without them, I could not possibly have accomplished it. I must pay a posthumous thanks to Richard Gordon Fitzgerald Uniacke, author of that Victorian Uniacke family history, a work that left a clear chronology and a record of documentary evidence later destroyed, even if he did not tell the full story. I also wish to thank the following for their assistance and advice: Jeremy Uniacke, Margaret Naylon, John Cunningham, Mary Clarke, Dr Raymond Gillespie, Dr David Dickson, Dr James McGuire, W. N. Osborough, Geraldine Tallon, the staff of the National Library of Ireland, the National Archives, the public library service, the manuscripts department of Trinity College Dublin and the Dublin Corporation archives. Finally, I am grateful to the team at Mercier Press for bringing this volume to its publishable state, and to my wife, Mary, and son, Robert, for their support from the very start.

Introduction

Most of the material in the introduction is dealt with in the following chapter notes, though it is important to refer to the 1641 Rebellion, an event that made an indelible mark on the Protestant psyche. It helped to influence attitudes at the time and over subsequent centuries. It is only right to record the facts – as I understand them to be – and let them speak for themselves.

The polemical writings of Sir John Temple, *The History of the Rebellion in Ireland* (London 1646), stirred strong emotions. The exact number of Protestant settlers killed by the Irish rebels is unknown: Temple reckoned it was over 150,000. This figure is too high according to Jane Ohlemeyer, 'Wars of Religion' in Bartlett and Jeffery (eds) *Military History of Ireland* (Cambridge 1996), who said the population could not have exceeded 200,000. William Petty put the death toll near 40,000. Historian Samuel R. Gardner in *History of England*, vol. X, pp. 64–9 (London 1883–84) estimated between 4,000 and 5,000 killed initially, with up to 25,000 being murdered or dying from starvation in the following three or four years. Nicholas Canny's chapter, 'What Really Happened in 1641?' in Jane Ohmleyer, ed., *Ireland From Independence to Occupation 1641–1660* (Cambridge 1996) describes how attacks on isolated homesteads were 'very gruesome affairs', but killings were rare enough, usually happening when occupants refused to leave their homes. He did note a pattern of torture, often to extract the location of hidden money.

Chapter One: 'Troublesome Times'

An important source was R. G. Fitzgerald Uniacke, who wrote the family history at the end of the nineteenth century published in the *Journal of the Cork Historical and Archaeological Society* (Cork 1894).

Two important sources for early Youghal are S. Hayman, *Memorials of Youghal: Ecclesiastical and Civil* (Youghal 1879, 1971) and Richard Caulfield, *Council Book of Youghal* (Guildford 1878).

Chapter Two: Innocent Blood

The first chapter is about Cromwell's campaign in Drogheda, a controversial episode in Irish history. The Jesuit historian Denis Murphy's *Cromwell in Ireland* (Dublin 1892) is a good narrative account, though admittedly coloured by nineteenth century Irish nationalist fervour. W. C. Abbott, *Cromwell's Speeches and Writings*, 4 vols (Cambridge Massachusetts 1939–47) is more analytical. J. G. Simms' article (*Irish Sword*, 1973–74) is detailed and meticulous. One of the most recent contributions is *Cromwell in Ireland* by James Scott Wheeler (Dublin 1999) a clear and readable account with interesting insights into military aspects of the campaign. C. H. Firth's *Cromwell's Army* (London 1902) is another essential authority on the period.

I do not enter the debate on whether Cromwell ordered the massacre of the entire population or killed soldiers after they had been granted quarter. I attempt to report the facts as agreed or reported by one side or the other. There are occasions where the puritan leader showed great acts of humanity. In her biography, *Cromwell: Our Chief of Men* (London 1973), Antonia Fraser portrays him as a complex individual. There is an unsettling ambiguity in the man who wrote about the 'righteous judgement of God upon those barbarous wretches who have imbued their hands with so much blood' whilst dismissing the deaths at Drogheda – revenge for 1641!

An essential textbook for understanding the half-century leading up to 1649 is Aidan Clarke, *The Old English in Ireland 1625–42* (London 1966).

The rumoured and anecdotal accounts of atrocities by Cromwell's forces – some of them utterly fantastic – are based on the relevant sections in Murphy. I have included them as popular folklore rather than historical facts that reflected widespread perception at the time and later. The arrival of refugees at Youghal after the revolt of the garrison in Cork is based on the *Memoirs of Lady Fanshawe* (London, 1830). The evidence of violence by soldiers comes from Cromwell's own writings, and suggests the disorder could have been quite widespread. Cromwell inspecting his troops is from an article in the *Journal of the Cork Historical and Archaeological Society*, 1894. It gives an account by someone who remembered an old man who was a boy in the winter of 1649–50, and saw Cromwell. The account also describes the funeral of General Jones. Murphy suggests Cromwell might have poisoned Jones. But there is little evidence, according to Archibald Kerr, in *An Ironside in Ireland: The Remarkable Career of Lieutenant-General Michael Jones* (London 1923). The description of Christmas festivities comes from Kevin Danaher, *The Year in Ireland* (Cork 1972). The war of words between Cromwell and the Catholic bishops comes from Cromwell's own writings (Abbott); Rinuccini Commentaries, Irish Manuscripts Commission (6 vols 1932–1936); the bishops' proclamations are reproduced in an appendix of Murphy's 'Cromwell in Ireland'.

Chapter Three: War ... Plague ... and Famine
The sources for Cromwell's spring campaign were chiefly Abbott, Murphy, Wheeler, and Vol. 3, *A New History of Ireland*.

There are numerous references to the plague that reached the country in July 1649 and was widespread by the following spring. Sources: *Diurnall of the Armies* 10–18 March 1650, p. 126; 18–25 March 1650, p. 131; Raymond Gillespie 'The Irish Economy at War' in Ohlmeyer, ed., *Ireland From Independence to Occupation 1641–1660*; TT (Thomaston Tracts, British Library London) E534 (29), Several Proceedings, 11–18 April 1650, p. 411, Cromwellian account of how local population were dying in large numbers. In her book, *A History of the Black Death in Ireland* (Stroud 2001), Maria Kelly describes the 1650 plague as the last great outbreak and 'one of the most destructive'. Her book deals chiefly with the fourteenth century outbreak, as do many of the other sources I consulted, such as *The Black Death* (London 1969) by

Philip Ziegler. Advances in medical science had not been great in the intervening centuries. Seventeenth century sources for public hygiene measures are readily available, and helped to reconstruct the experience of Youghal during this outbreak. After the plague, the country was visited by famine (see Robert Dunlop, *Ireland Under the Commonwealth*, Manchester 1913). In his survey of 1652, William Petty, in *The Political Anatomy of Ireland* (London 1672), estimated the Irish population to be 850,000, and that 616,000 had perished since 1641. See *A New History of Ireland*, Vol. 3, p. 357; Wheeler, pp. 224–227; *The Great Irish Famine*, ed., Cathal Poirteir (Cork 1995) pp. 51–52, chapter by David Dickson, 'The Other Great Irish Famine'. Dickson describes the mid seventeenth century crisis as 'tantalisingly opaque'. For this reason I have relied upon the voluminous accounts of The Great Famine of 1845–47 to recreate the harrowing picture of human suffering, as the nineteenth century crisis is much better documented than the tragedy 200 years before.

Chapter Four: … Unsettling of a Nation …
The title of the chapter is taken from the pamphlet *The Great Case of Transplantation in Ireland Discussed* by Vincent Gookin (London 1655). For a brief summary of the Cromwellian settlement read Wheeler, pp. 227–30. On the nature and severity of the legislation see Karl Bottigheimer *English Money and Irish Land* (Oxford 1971), pp. 127–8; the practical problems of attracting new settlers, S. R. Gardiner 'The Transplantation to Connaught', *English Historical Review* 1899, pp. 733–4; T. C. Barnard 'Planters and Policy in Cromwellian Ireland', *Past and Present*, No. 61 (November 1973), pp. 32–3, pp. 68–9; soldiers selling debentures see Bottigheimer, *English Money and Irish Land*, p. 140. The list of Youghal citizens to forfeit their lands is from J. O'Hart, *Irish Landed Gentry When Cromwell Came to Ireland* (Dublin 1883). The Uniackes' petition against being transplanted is an example of how the legal process slowed down the entire settlement policy. The petition is reproduced from Fitzgerald Uniacke's family history. Chapter three, Barnard's *Cromwellian Ireland* is an excellent analysis of the economy during the 1650s. Also read Samuel Hayman 'The Local Coinage of Youghal', *Journal of the Kilkenny and Southeast of Ireland Archaeological Society*, 1858–9 pp. 224–31; and W. A. Seaby 'A Bond for Issuers of Youghal Tokens', *Journal of the Royal Society of Antiquaries of Ireland*, 1972, p. 161. According to Fitzgerald Uniacke the family had its petition heard on 5 August 1656 and the surviving copy of the petition outlines the Uniacke case. Other sources are: J. P. Prendergast, *The*

Cromwellian Settlement of Ireland (London 1865, repr. 1996), pp. 231–233; Dunlop, pp. ii, 467, 535, 604–5, 613, 618.

The Uniackes never moved to Muskerry or Barrymore – they stayed in Youghal. Details of the forfeitures are found in Fitzgerald Uniacke, and in *Submissions to the 1663 Court of Claims*, Geraldine Tallon (Dublin 1999). The family was still in the town in 1659, see Seamus Pender, ed., *A 'Census' of Ireland circa 1659* (Dublin 1939). It seems most likely that the Uniackes remained in Youghal and managed the estates for the new landlords. The text for the Oath of Abjuration is taken from *Acts and Ordinances of the Interregnum*, C. H. Firth and R. S. Rait (London 1911).

Chapter Five: Restoration of Hope
I am greatly indebted to the scholarly yet compact work of Patrick J. Corish, *The Catholic Communities in the 17th and 18th Centuries* (Dublin 1981). An authority on ecclesiastical history, the late Fr Corish brought together all the disparate sources for this complex and often confused period. The book is a brilliant illumination of the times. It helped me understand the issues and religious struggles of Catholics such as Thomas Uniacke. Father Jasper Galwan is mentioned in the will of Maurice Uniacke, and was no doubt a close friend of the Uniackes. The first order for the transplantation of 'priests and friars' was made in January 1655. All religious had to sign an undertaking they would not return to Ireland. Aubrey Gwynn (writing in the Irish quarterly review, *Studies*, xx, Dublin 1931 pp. 291–305) gives a grim account of the conditions for indentured slaves. The authorities mistrusted priests – they could organise the Irish to rebel, so were frequently deported, permitted to go to anywhere outside the English Commonwealth established by Cromwell. Thomas Uniacke witnessed or heard of harrowing scenes as the country sunk into despair. His perceptions would also have been formed by secondhand accounts, as described by one of his contemporaries: 'Great multitudes of poor [are] swarming in all parts of this nation …' (Dunlop, pp. ii, 340). Later Dunlop records that Lord Broghill was ordered to round up all those who could not support themselves, to be made ready for transportation. The Rinuccini Commentaries give a description: 'Nothing is more painful than to witness the shipment of those exiles, the father separated from his child, brother from brother, sister from sister, spouse from spouse … At one place we see the sons of noble families, the hope and consolation of their aged parents, youths delicately reared and carefully educated, who are not only robbed of every chance of their

more valuable clothes, receiving instead tattered rags, and are flogged with rods and branded like sheep on skin and flesh, and then driven among the crowd on board these infamous transportation ships.' The account tells of young maidens being dragged to the ships, 'piercing heaven with their shrieks'. Or the case of a wife pleading with the authorities that she be sold into slavery along with her husband. Of course, much of these stories are anecdotal. For example, the historian J. W. Blake argues that there are no shipping records extant to prove, one way or the other, the scale of transplantation: 'It is by no means easy to collate these two disparate types of evidence, and to prove either that government plans for transplantation were actually carried out, or that particular transportation ships actually left Ireland, crossed the Atlantic, and reached their colonial destinations (Transplantation from Ireland to America, *IHS*, March 1943, pp. 267–81).

Chapter Six: A Family Divided
The only reference to James Uniacke being in Trinity comes from Fitzgerald Uniacke's history. There are abundant accounts of Ireland from the period – Thomas Dinely, William Brereton, John Dunton, John Stevens. Modern authors of help to my research were George O'Brien, *Economic History of Ireland in the Seventeenth Century* (Dublin 1919), Edward McLysaght, *Irish Life in the Seventeenth Century* (Cork 1950), Maurice Craig, *Dublin 1660–1860* (Dublin 1969), L. M. Cullen, *Life in Ireland* (London/New York 1968) and Mairead Dunlevy, *Dress in Ireland* (London 1989). The volume of works available enabled me to create a picture of the time. Taylor/Skinner, *Maps of the Roads of Ireland* (London 1776), helped me retrace the likely route that James Uniacke took to Dublin. The second part of the chapter covers the witch trial of Florence Newton in Youghal, which comes from Rev St John D. Seymour *Witchcraft and Demonology in Ireland* (Dublin 1913).

Chapter Seven: A Plea For Justice
In addition to Fitzgerald Uniacke, there are references to James Uniacke acting in a legal capacity for Youghal Corporation. My main sources for the Court of Claims were L. J. Arnold 'The Irish Court of Claims of 1663' in *Irish Historical Studies*, November 1985, and his book *The Restoration Land Settlement in County Dublin* (Dublin 1993). The date of the Uniacke hearing and other details is given in the *Nineteenth Report of the Deputy Keeper of Public Records*. The petition by the Uniackes in 1663 is preserved in submissions to the court and held in Armagh Public Library. I acknowledge the permission of the Irish

Manuscripts Commission to quote from its forthcoming publication of Geraldine Tallon's edition of the Court of Claims papers. The later legal action taken by Thomas Uniacke comes from Fitzgerald Uniacke, and seems to be the only surviving copy of the documents being discussed.

Chapter Eight: Calm Between Storms

Fitzgerald Uniacke states that James Uniacke firmly established himself in Dublin, making a commercial success of his legal training. We know very little about his wife, Mary Neale. But the name is frequent in Dublin parish records. A narrowing down of the dates in the Dublin Corporation Archives makes it most likely, in my opinion, that she was the daughter of James Neale. Fitzgerald Uniacke records that they were married in St Werburgh parish. Fitzgerald Uniacke found records of a James Uniacke's connection with Youghal in the Council Book. There is evidence that Thomas Uniacke borrowed extensively during this period. Fitzgerald Uniacke quotes one example, where he borrowed £100 from his brother, James. But I came across a second £100 loan (National Archives of Ireland 1135/24 Beresford papers). In both cases Thomas and his mother had to put up property as collateral. The papers also show him paying back a £243 loan to a Matthew Jones. Thomas also leased land from the Earl of Cork (Fitzgerald Uniacke). The source for the enormous £2,000 loan comes from the *The Irish Staple Statute Books 1596–1687*, ed. Jane Ohlemeyer and Eamonn Ó Ciardha (Dublin 1988). David Dickson's chapter in *Cork: History and Society* (Dublin 1993), 'Butter Comes to Market: The Origins of Commercial Dairying in County Cork', gives an excellent insight into the agricultural economy in the second half of the seventeenth century. The *Council Book* gives a glimpse of an increasingly sectarian society – even if the attitude to Catholics was relatively relaxed – with the corporation ordering the closure of the gates during Sunday services. A good overview of the religious tension of the period came from *The War of Religions*, Brendan Fitzpatrick (Dublin 1988). Fitzgerald Uniacke tells us James Uniacke resided in Back Lane and made a considerable fortune. The details of James' will are from the family history. Dublin Corporation archives also show James was a freeman of Dublin and had a stationery business in the capital.

Chapter Nine: A Catholic King

The institutional and religious changes introduced on the accession of James II are well documented and researched by historians. An important contemporaneous account is *The State of Protestants in Ireland*

under the Late King James (London 1691). Hayman gives some indication of the local effect in Youghal: 'During the War of Succession,
Youghal had its full share of religious turmoil. Its Protestant inhabitants
were scattered. Some were imprisoned and some driven into exile.
Heavy penalties were laid on all. In the parish church, the minister
(Gilbert Heathcote) was no longer permitted to officiate; and the ritual
of the Church of Rome was resumed within its walls.' In this chapter,
we get the first glimpse of Thomas Uniacke Junior from Fitzgerald
Uniacke and also an interesting snippet of Eleanor Uniacke petition-
ing the king to give her husband a job (Treasury Irish Books).

Chapter Ten: 'The Pretend Parliament'
The two main sources for chapter ten were *The Patriot Parliament of
1689* by Thomas Davis, ed. C. Gavin Duffy (London 1893) and the
authoritative historian J. G. Simms, The *Jacobite Parliament of 1689*
Dublin Historical Association (1966).

Chapter Eleven: Battle of the Boyne
The general sources for this chapter included 'Kings in Conflict' in *The
Fate of Ireland*, ed. Robert Sheppard (London 1990) and *Irish Battles*,
G. A. Hayes-McCoy (London 1969). Fitzgerald Uniacke tells us that
James Uniacke Junior fought at the Battle of the Boyne 'commanding
a troop of men'. Most of the contemporaneous accounts come from
Williamite sources. Most prominent among them, George Story, A *True
And Impartial History of the Wars in Ireland* (London 1691) and A *Conti-
nuation of the Impartial History of the Wars in Ireland* (London 1693); *The
Diary of Thomas Bellingham* (London 1908) gives precise details of
weather conditions, helping to re-create the scene; *The Records of the
Inniskilling Dragoons* (London 1909), E. S. Jackson.

Chapter Twelve: The Aftermath
A useful and informative biography of Patrick Sarsfield is *Patrick Sarsfield and the Williamite War* by Piers Wauchope (Dublin 1992). *The
Council Book of Youghal* and the later history of the county by Charles
Smith give some indication of the aftermath of the battle of the Boyne
and its effect on the Uniackes and other Catholic gentry. These sources
give a picture of what happened in the locality during the weeks and
months following. The continuation of the war on to the decisive
battle at Aughrim and the Treaty of Limerick is well covered by historians. Again, the continuation of Story's *Impartial History* is a primary
source. Hayes-McCoy's *Irish Battles* deals extensively with Aughrim.

Chapter Thirteen: The Outlawed

J. G. Simms, *The Williamite Confiscation in Ireland 1690–1703* (London 1956) was an essential text, especially chapters three and seven. James I. McGuire's essay in *Penal Era and Golden Age: Essays in Irish History 1690–1800*, eds, T. Bartlett and D. Hayton (Belfast 1979) gives a detailed analysis of Sydney's time as Lord Lieutenant from the political perspective, and of the accusation that he was sympathetic to Catholics. The *Dictionary of National Biography* provides a detailed overview of the character and life of Romney. In the introduction to the *Diary of the Time of Charles II by Henry Sydney*, R. W. Blencowe offers a useful insight into Sydney, and his treatment of his mistress Mrs Whortley. Regarding Sydney's affair with Margaret Uniacke, there was anecdotal evidence that the Margaret in question was the daughter of Catholic Thomas Uniacke of Youghal, a point that seems to be confirmed by Simms (*The Williamite Confiscations*, pp. 78–79). A *New History of Ireland 1690–1800*, Vol. 4 (1986), says Sydney was 'under the influence of a Catholic mistress', though I was never able to find any source for this. When I checked the manuscripts of the books appended to the parliamentary commission on forfeitures (MS N1. 3.), I found that Margaret Uniacke is mentioned at several points as having received money from Catholic gentry. But in the *Book of Pardons* Thomas Uniacke is described as her uncle, making her the daughter of James Uniacke, the solicitor. The confusion arises because there were two Margarets, cousins. This makes more sense as – living in Dublin and being in the social elite – James' daughter would have been invited to events in Dublin Castle; she almost certainly met Sydney in this way.

In trying to recreate a picture of Dublin Castle as the young Uniacke ladies entered society, the following publications helped: *Champagne and Silver Buckles, The Viceregal Court at Dublin Castle*, Joseph Robbins (Dublin 2001); *Dublin Castle – Historical Background and Guide*, J. B. Maguire (Dublin 1992); *Illustrated Encyclopaedia of Costumes and Fashion*, Jack Cassin-Scott (Dorset 1986); *Chronicle of Western Costume*, John Peacock (London 1991); *Fashion in Costume 1200–2000*, Joan Nunn (London 1984).

Taking Sydney's character and the fact that Margaret Uniacke was identified in *The Report of the Commissioners Appointed by Parliament to Inquire into the Irish Forfeitures* (London 1700) as the most pertinent examples of corruption, whereby pardons were granted for money, we can conclude in the general sense that they were lovers.

Chapter Fourteen: The Conformed

Fitzgerald Uniacke was the source for much of the biographical history in this chapter, and his notebook retains original copies of items such young James' Uniacke's commission as a coronet in the dragoons. The history also reproduces the litigation taken by Thomas Uniacke against his father.

Epilogue

Fitzgerald Uniacke also provided much of the material for the epilogue. Two other publications following the fortunes of the family are: *Richard John Uniacke (1753–1830)*, *The Old Attorney General*, by B. Cuthbertson (Halifax, Canada, 1980) and *Discovery of the Brisbane River, 1823, Oxley, Uniacke and Pamphlet 175 Years in Retropect*, by Marc Serge Riviére (Brisbane, Australia, 1998).

Bibliography

Abbott, W. C., *Cromwell's Speeches and Writings* (Cambridge Massachusetts 1939–47)

Arnold, L. J., *The Restoration Land Settlement in County Dublin* (Dublin 1993)

Arnold, L. J., 'The Irish Court of Claims of 1663', *Irish Historical Studies* (November 1985)

Barnard, T. C., *Cromwellian Ireland: English Government and Reform in Ireland 1649–1660* (Oxford 1975)

Barnard, T. C., 'Planters and Policy in Cromwellian Ireland', *Past and Present*, No. 61 (November 1973)

Beckett, J. C., *Making of Modern Ireland 1603–1923* (London 1966)

Bellingham, Thomas, *Diaries* (London 1908)

Blake, J. W., 'Transplantation from Ireland to America', *Irish Historical Studies* (March 1943)

Blencowe, R. W., ed., *Diary of the Time of Charles II by Henry Sydney* (London 1843)

Bottigheimer, Karl, *English Money and Irish Land* (Oxford 1971)

Canny, Nicholas, 'What Really Happened in 1641?' in Jane Ohlemeyer, ed., *Ireland From Independence to Occupation 1641–1660* (Cambridge 1996)

Cassin-Scott, Jack, *Illustrated Encyclopaedia of Costume and Fashion* (Dorset 1986)

Caulfield, Richard, *Council Book of Youghal* (Guildford 1878)

Clarke, Aidan, *The Old English in Ireland 1625–42* (London 1966)

Corish, Patrick J., *The Catholic Community in the 17th and 18th Centuries* (Dublin 1981)

Craig, Maurice, *Dublin 1660–1860* (Dublin 1969)

Cullen, L. M., *Life in Ireland* (London/New York 1968)

Cuthbertson, B., *Richard John Uniacke (1753–1830), The Old Attorney General* (Halifax, Canada 1980)

Danaher, Kevin, *The Year in Ireland* (Cork 1972)

Davis, Thomas, ed., *The Patriot Parliament of 1689* (London 1893)

Dickson, David, 'Butter Comes to Market: The Origins of Commercial Dairying in County Cork' in O'Flanagan, Patrick and Buttimer, Neil, eds, *Cork: History and Society* (Dublin 1993)

Dickson, David, *New Foundations: Ireland 1660–1800* (Dublin 1987)

Dickson, David, 'The Other Great Irish Famine' in Póirtéir, Cathal, ed., *The Great Irish Famine* (Cork 1995)

Dunleavy, Mairead, *Dress in Ireland* (London 1989)

Dunlop, Robert, *Ireland Under the Commonwealth* (Manchester 1913)

Falkiner, C. L., *Illustrations of Irish History and Biography* (London 1902)

Fanshawe, Lady, *Memoirs of Lady Fanshawe* (London 1830)

Firth, C. H., *Cromwell's Army* (London 1902)

Firth, C. H. and Rait, R. S., eds., *Acts and Ordinances of the Interregnum* (London 1911)

Fitzgerald Uniacke, R. G., 'The Uniackes of Youghal', *Journal of the Cork Historical and Archaeological Society* (Cork 1894)

Fitzpatrick, Brendan, *The War of Religions* (Dublin 1988)

Foster, R. F., *Modern Ireland 1600–1972* (London 1988)

Frazer, Antonia, *Cromwell: Our Chief of Men* (London 1973)

Gardner, Samuel R., *History of England* (London 1883–84)

Gardner, Samuel R., 'The Transplantation to Connaught', *English Historical Review* (1899)

Gillespie, Raymond, 'The Irish Economy at War' in Ohlemeyer, Jane, ed., *Ireland From Independence to Occupation 1641–1660* (Cambridge 1996)

Gookin, Vincent, *The Great Case of Transplantation in Ireland Discussed* (London 1655)

Hayes-McCoy, G. A., *Irish Battles* (London 1969)

Hayman, S., *Memorials of Youghal: Ecclesiastical and Civil* (Youghal 1879, 1971)

Hayman, S., 'Local Coinage of Youghal', *Journal of the Kilkenny and Southeast Archaeological Society* (1858–59)

Jackson, E. S., *The Records of the Inniskilling Dragoons* (London 1909)

Kelly, Maria, *A History of the Black Death in Ireland* (Stroud 2001)

Kerr, Archibald, *An Ironside in Ireland: The Remarkable Career of Lieutenant-General Michael Jones* (London 1923)

Maguire, J. B., *Dublin Castle – Historical Background and Guide* (Dublin 1992)

McGuire, James I., 'The Irish Parliament of 1692' in Bartlett T. and Hayton, D. eds, *Penal Era and Golden Age: Essays in Irish History 1690–1800* (Belfast 1979)

McLysaght, Edward, *Irish Life in the Seventeenth Century* (Cork 1950)

Moody, T. W., Martin, F. X., Byrne, F. J., eds, *A New History of Ireland, vol iii: Early Modern Ireland 1534–1691* (Oxford 1976)

Moody, T. W., Martin, F. X., *The Course of Irish History* (Cork 1967)

Moody, T. W. and Vaughan, W. E., eds, *A New History of Ireland, vol iv: 1691–1800* (Oxford 1986)

Murphy, Denis, *Cromwell in Ireland* (Dublin 1892)

Nunn, Joan, *Fashion in Costume 1200–2000* (London 1984)

O'Brien, George, *Economic History of Ireland in the Seventeenth Century* (Dublin 1919)

O'Hart, J., *Irish Landed Gentry When Cromwell Came to Ireland* (Dublin 1883)

Ohlemeyer, Jane and Ó Ciardha, Eamonn, eds, *Staple Statute Books 1596–1687* (Dublin 1998)

Ohlemeyer, Jane, 'Wars of Religion' in Bartlett and Jeffery (eds) *Military History of Ireland* (Cambridge 1996)

Peacock, John, *Chronicles of Western Costume* (London 1991)

Pender, Seamus, ed., *A Census of Ireland Circa 1659* (Dublin 1939)

Petty, William, *The Political Anatomy of Ireland* (London 1672)

Prendergast, J. P., *The Cromwellian Settlement of Ireland* (London 1865)

Report of the Commission Appointed by Parliament to Inquire into the Irish Forfeitures (London 1700).

Report (19th) of the Deputy Keeper of Public Records (Dublin)

Riviére, Marc Serge, *Discovery of the Brisbane River, 1823, Oxley, Uniacke and Pamphlet 175 Years in Retropect* (Brisbane 1998)

Robbins, Joseph, *Champagne and Silver Buckles: The Viceregal Court at Dublin Castle* (Dublin 2001)

Seaby, W. A., 'A Bond of Issuers of Youghal Tokens', *Journal of the Royal Society of Antiquaries of Ireland* (1972)

Seymour, Rev. St John D., *Witchcraft and Demonology in Ireland* (Dublin 1913)

Sheppard, Robert, *The Fate of Ireland* (London 1990)

Simms, J. G., *The Williamite Confiscations in Ireland* (London 1956)

Story, George, *A True And Impartial History of the Wars in Ireland* (London 1691)

Tallon, Geraldine, ed., *Court of Claims Papers* (Irish Manuscripts Commission: publication summer 2004)

Taylor George, Skinner, Andrew, *Maps of the Roads of Ireland* (London 1776)

Temple, Sir John, *The History of the Rebellion in Ireland* (London 1646)

Wauchope, Piers, *Patrick Sarsfield and the Irish Williamite Wars* (Dublin 1992)

Wheeler, James Scott, *Cromwell in Ireland* (Dublin 1999)

Ziegler, Philip, *The Black Death* (London 1969)

Also available from
Mercier Press

A Short History of Orangeism
Kevin Haddick-Flynn

Tracing the development of the Orange tradition from its beginnings during the Williamite War (1688–91) to the present day, this book comprehensively covers all the main events and personalities. It provides information on such little known organisations as the Royal Black Preceptory and the Royal Arch Purple Order, as well as institutions like the Apprentice Boys of Derry.

Military campaigns and rebellions are set against a background of intrigue and infighting; anti-Catholic rhetoric is matched with anti-Orange polemic. This compelling book narrates the history of a quasi-Masonic organisation and looks at its rituals and traditions.

The Great Irish Famine
Edited by Cathal Póirtéir

This is the most wide-ranging series of essays ever published on the Great Irish Famine and has proved to be of lasting interest to the general reader. Leading historians, economists, geographers – from Ireland, Britain and the United States – have assembled the most up-to-date research from a wide spectrum of disciplines, including medicine, folklore and literature, to give the fullest account yet of the background and consequences of the Famine.

THE COURSE OF IRISH HISTORY
Edited by T. W. Moody and F. X. Martin

A revised and enlarged version of this classic book provides a rapid short survey, with geographical introduction, of the whole course of Ireland's history. Based on a series of television programmes, it is designed to be both popular and authoritative, concise but comprehensive, highly selective but balanced and fair-minded, critical but constructive and sympathetic. A distinctive feature is its wealth of illustrations.

THE LEGACY OF HISTORY
Martin Mansergh

These essays describe the origins of the conflicts and crises in Irish history, as well as highlighting concerns for the future. The author suggests the historical significance of much that has been achieved in recent years.

Subjects dealt with include the Battle of Kinsale, the resonances of the Treaty of Limerick in the current Northern peace process, the commemoration of the rebellions of 1798 and 1848, the legacy of Wolfe Tone and the patriotism of Pádraic Pearse and Roger Casement.

SARSFIELD AND THE JACOBITES
Kevin Haddick-Flynn

The first book written on Patrick Sarsfield by an Irishman in over 100 years, Sarsfield and the Jacobites is a military biography set against the background of the 'Glorious Revolution' and the Williamite War (1688–1691).

It examines Sarsfield's military career in detail, with special focus on his role as the most outstanding Irish soldier of the Williamite War.